William Henry
Library

Blind Victory

By the same Author

Freedom and Capital

Blind Victory

a study in
income, wealth and power

DAVID HOWELL

HAMISH HAMILTON
London

First published in Great Britain 1986
by Hamish Hamilton Ltd
Garden House, 57–59 Long Acre, London WC2E 9JZ

British Library Cataloguing in Publication Data

Howell, David. *1936–*
    Blind victory: a study in income,
    wealth and power.
    1. Great Britain—Economic policy—1945–
    I. Title
    330.941'0858   HC256.6
    ISBN 0–241–11743–7

Typeset by Input Typesetting Ltd, London
Printed and bound in Great Britain by
Billing & Sons Ltd, Worcester

To Davina

'Above all, the mass of society have commonsense, which the learned in all ages want.'

'The most sensible people to be met with in society are men of business and the world, who argue from what they see and know, instead of spinning cobweb distinctions of what things ought to be.'

William Hazlitt in his essay 'On the Ignorance of the Learned'

'But, chiefly, do not let us overestimate the importance of the economic problem, or sacrifice to its supposed necessities other matters of greater and more permanent significance. It should be a matter for specialists – like dentistry. If economists could manage to get themselves thought of as humble, competent people, on a level with dentists, that would be splendid!'

J. M. Keynes, 'Economic Possibilities for our Grandchildren'.

Contents

Preface

I hope that this will be regarded as an optimistic and cheerful book and not another moan about what is wrong with Britain. We have reached a very obvious milestone along the path of public affairs and it seems only sensible to pause, take out the maps and see where we are, the better to travel the next stage.

However, this is not at all a book of prophecy or futurology. Most of the trends and changes of outlook with which its is concerned are already well-established and have been so for some time. The question, of course – and one which is addressed in these pages – is whether the news of the new situation has percolated through to the centres of policy-making and government and whether in those quarters the real significance of what is really happening is still being missed or has now been grasped.

On the whole, my judgment, as the reader will see, is that far more of the message about the now drastically altered pattern of life and work in our society is getting through to those who settle public priorities than we might have dared hope a few years back, although there is a long way still to go and much for the present Government in Britain to do – not just by way of particular measures but also in mobilising its intellectual energies and providing a coherent setting for its aims and action.

I argue that the full import of the transformation that has occurred in the character of both the national and international economy, and therefore in the way advanced societies behave and governments should respond, has been nothing like fully appreciated. State collectivism has been completely defeated and outmoded and its arguments scattered. But the understandings, insights and policies required to make sense of the successor order, to explain a world which is both less controllable from the centre and less in need of such control, are by no means yet in place. That is what I mean by saying, through the title of this book, that the victory over past orthodoxy in our society has been a blind one, in which the new intellectual masters of the field do not seem to have entirely realised how their conquest has come about or what now to do with it.

This is the opportunity for me to thank some of those on whom I have leant in preparing this volume. I owe a debt to Stephen Breyer who encouraged me to start writing, to David Wolfson who talked some of the ideas through with me, to Professor Charles Handy who also encouraged me and whose understanding of the employment issue is so vastly superior to most people's and to John Pinder and all the other staff at the Policy Studies Institute who put up with me for a year or so and let me weary them.

I should also express my gratitude – although this may surprise the recipients – to those towering tutors who taught me economics at Cambridge and opened my eyes fully to the fragile foundations and unscientific nature of the subject. I refer to teachers like Nicholas Kaldor and Robin Marris, amongst many other great figures, who if they remember me at all, probably shake their heads at my deviant course, but from whom it was a life-time privilege to learn. For all my deep disagreement with these chief apostles of Keynes, and with their political outlook in many cases, I remain an unrepentant monetary Keynesian.

A word of thanks, too, to my Parliamentary friends and colleagues who, contrary to the stereotype and to the impression conveyed by the broadcasting of Parliamentary proceedings in the Chamber, constitute a lively and endlessly stimulating intellectual fellowship with whom it is a mighty privilege to work and mix daily. I should also thank my friends at the international brokers, Savory Milln, whose zest and calm business realism provide a constantly useful antidote to some of the hothouse tendencies of Westminster politics.

Above all I need to thank my wife, Davina, and my family, for both encouraging me endlessly and putting up with the hell of an author in the home. To them I owe the largest debt of all. Needless to say, the words, thoughts and views herein are my own and no one else is to blame.

David Howell
Pimlico, March 1986.

PART I

The New Landscape

'He that will not apply new remedies must expect new evils; for time is the greatest innovator.'

Francis Bacon

CHAPTER 1

Old Problems

For politicians, like everyone else, the world moves on. Old arguments die away and new concerns grow. We reach the mountain ridge and the valley beyond which we imagined unfolds at our feet, but somehow it looks different from what we expected and new mountains rise ahead.

The debates which raged in the 1970s in Britain, especially those between the Keynesians and the monetarists which were at their peak when I joined Mrs Thatcher's first Cabinet in 1979, and which seemed so central to our problems, already appear jaded and less connected with the terrain we can now see unfolding immediately before us.

The basic question is admittedly still the same. Can economic life 'adjust'? That was also the question in the 1930s when people asked whether free economies could adjust to violent business cycles, badly working markets and heavy concentrations of wealth. The classical economists said they would, eventually. Markets could be made to work. Keynes said they couldn't and that high level and bold intervention in the national economy was necessary. He tore to bits the advocates of small-scale reforms, and adjustments.[1]

The argument is still about adjustment. How does Britain adjust to the shattering impact of new technology and how does it adjust to the advent, the growth and then the gradual decline of North Sea oil? But it is the kind of adjustment which people seem to have in mind which has changed so greatly, not only since the thirties and the immediate post-war era, but again, and on an enormous scale, since the seventies as well.

The question of the future of work itself is replacing the familiar discussion about how to return to full employment

1. See in particular, the Appendix to Chapter 19 of *The General Theory*, and also the brief Chapter 1, when Keynes is emphatic on the point that he is indeed offering a *general* theory and not another set of postulates which only applied, he claimed, to a special case.

without inflation. Longstanding worries about Britain's struggling traditional industries are now being edged aside by the realisation that not just the old empires of coal, iron and steam but the very definitions of industries which thrived in the thirties and fifties are being blurred, miniaturised and fragmented into a new jigsaw by the new information technology which a decade ago still belonged to futurology. The microprocessor has long since begun to impose on us an entirely new industrial structure.

The arguments about state intervention and state ownership are being overtaken as the nature of the state itself changes and old patterns of power dissolve. Even if the centre still wanted to control and manage the great aggregates of society, like demand, or investment, or the money supply, those aggregates have crumbled away, leaving governments with an increasingly hollow husk of knowledge and information about what is actually going on in our looser and more disaggregated society – and therefore much less able to influence and control affairs.

Big solid sectors, classes and Blue Book categories, the chunky raw material of the centralists, the state socialists, as well as the Keynesian demand managers, are melting, mingling and dissolving. The 'soft' economy, in which more and more people are engaged in knowledge-based industries and services, and in which physical manufacturing employs fewer and is less concentrated, has started to assume new characteristics which baffle economic planners. We seem to have entered an era in which economic cycles move in smaller waves and in which a new climate of stability, without central intervention, may be attainable. In this sense, therefore, the anti-collectivists and the anti-statists has won hands down. The unplanners have defeated the planners completely. There has to be less government because more government is becoming unnecessary and unworkable. The corporatists, who rested their thinking on big unionism, big government, big finance and big industry, are seeing their edifice collapse not because they have lost some temporary political power struggle (or because some other clique has won it), but because this degree of centralism has simply become outdated. The computer and micro-electronic communications disperse power and knowledge, and therefore traditional political formations, just as they disperse and alter industrial and commercial activity.

So a new business landscape has emerged, and therefore a

new political landscape as well. Smaller enterprises, much more self-employment and home-based work and a revival of family undertakings (shades of society before the Industrial Revolution created an urban working class and its politics), all have prominence on this new scene. They do not do so because the politicians have planned it but because people find this new pattern more comfortable, flexible and workable, and because smaller organisations and groupings have now gained the power and the access to information which could only be found at mass and nationwide levels earlier.

This huge defeat of centralism is not just confined to Britain. It is worldwide. China's quarter of the human race has recognised and embraced the trend away from central planning and towards dispersed, market-based decision-making. Even the tightest tyrannies are finding themselves cracked open both by the demand for more decentralisation and by telecommunications and satellite technology as the worried masters of the old Soviet empire now evidently realise.

The most successful and prospering societies seem to be those which have the most atomised, loose and supple industrial structures – those which float on a sea of sub-contractors, micro-businesses and only half-visible black-grey economic activity. This is not at all the same thing as saying that rugged individualism rules or that text-book market economics has prevailed or that the classical economists have won after all. No one would put Japan, for example, in that category. It is rather that a mosaic structure of small cells and groupings, a composition of what the French call 'groupuscules' (to which Alvin Toffler has also referred)[1], is becoming a more natural and stronger social pattern than the unnatural centralised systems and class organisations upon which Marxian analysis rested and round which our politics have been built. There are signs on all sides in the advanced societies of a new kind of work ethic emerging, resting neither on individual self-help nor on collectivism, but on something in between. James Robertson calls this the ethic of co-operative self-reliance, and we shall have much more to say about it.[2]

---

1. 'An Appointment with the Future' *Sunday Times*, May 19, 1985.
2. '*Future Work*', page 109, Gower/Temple Smith, 1985.

Blind Victory

But if all this has been a kind of intellectual victory for the libertarians and the political right, it is in acute danger of being a blind one, a victory of which the consequences are not comprehended, in short a victory without a purpose. State socialism and its satrapies may have become discredited and disjointed but what replaces them? What are the philosophies, the binding themes, which will give this new pattern some reasonable coherence and stability?

This was the question which concerned some of us in Britain in the seventies as we looked forward towards the inevitable demise of collectivism and the fragmentation of its traditional trade union political support in Britain. In its place, we hoped for a process by which the excluded 'middle classes' would reassert themselves, spreading their style and values to embrace just about everybody – a new triumph of the bourgeoisie, suspicious of state action, thinking small, recognising specific social obligation in place of the generalised compassion of the welfare state.[1] The 'macro' aspects of economic and social policy, we argued, could more or less be left on automatic pilot, with sound, non-inflationary finance, tightly controlled money supply and balanced budgets. On the 'micro' side, competition and market economics would reign. Markets would work as they had not worked in the 1920s. The economy would 'adjust'. Taxes would come down, deregulation would spread, the state industrial empires would be dismantled and privatised, and widespread capital-ownership would replace concentrated monopoly ownership. These would be the foundations of the property-owning democracy – a liberation from the power of the socialist state.

The Crumbling Assumptions

Some of this pattern has begun to take shape. But now that we can peer further ahead from the platform of the mid-eighties we find that the unfolding landscape has some new and unexpected contours as well. First, micro-electronics have 'arrived' at vastly greater speed than the politicians anticipated. Policymaking and political debate have barely begun to catch up with the fact of the soft economy, the new and entirely different

1. See, for instance, my book, *Freedom and Capital*, Blackwell, 1980.

rules by which it is beginning to operate, and the new work arrangements and lifestyles it imposes.

Second, unemployment has passed through the stage of being a cyclical or structural phenomenon which 'supply-side' economics would straighten out in due course. Over the hill it now begins to look like only one part of a much larger condition in which whole-life patterns of both work and leisure are changing, in which full-time paid employment is no longer the sole determinant of income, in which multi-occupations and part-time activities proliferate and in which all the social policies of the state, geared to a quite different age, have to be revised.

Third, the whole idea of education is becoming stretched and altered in a way that takes it far beyond the educationalists' debates of a decade ago. Learning and work are becoming more inter-mingled. People now see learning, training and the acquisition of new skills as just as much a part of a satisfying pattern of living as full-time employment. They are regarded as something which should be available not just at the beginning of the working life, but throughout and well beyond it, into the still active seventies and even eighties.

Nor are people so content as they were to see their children educated just as *employees*. The same understanding that there is more to work and life than simple employee status, that people should be free to work independently and in a rhythm of their own choosing, is spreading to views about what parents want for their children out of education. The 'privileges' of further education and instruction in the arts of self-reliance and self-occupation throughout life are now quite suddenly expected to be provided on a mass scale, for all children at all levels of ability, rather in the way that governments were previously expected to provide full-time employment for all in the 1950s and 1960s.

Fourth, the anti-centralism which was foreseen has certainly blossomed in society. However, it has produced not just a climate hostile to central planning and state socialism, but all sorts of other tensions as well. Local community concern, and self-confidence and assertiveness, have grown strongly. The power of central government has been directly challenged. It could well be that we are at the beginning of a Hundred Years War between central and local government forces inside the modern nation states, reviving ancient divisions and bitter-

nesses which the old centralised industrial state had success-
fully suppressed.

Fifth, decentralisation has also been at work in the very heart
of the industrial process. Not only has the impact of micro-
electronics flattened the management pyramid and permitted
vastly greater delegation of responsibilities within the firm, it
has allowed manufacturers to take a completely new attitude
towards the structure of their operations. The large centralised
operation, exerting tight control and supplying common
services to numerous branches, is simply ceasing to be the most
logical way of organising economic activity. The economics of
scale have been overwhelmed by the diseconomies, and by the
alternative and fast-growing economies of miniaturisation and
smaller units, and of sub-contracting outside the factory wher-
ever possible. The British economy has traditionally been
concentrated and therefore is particularly susceptible to these
new influences. Nowhere have they been more evident than in
the heavily centralised state sector where the whole philosophy
of the nationalised industries have always been, quite deliberately, one of gathering in activities to the centre, of co-ordinating and rationalising on a national scale in line with orthodox
management and employment conceptions of the age in which
they were set up (mostly after the Second World War).

Thus, quite aside from the enthusiasm of the Conservative
Government for privatisation and dismantling the state industrial sector (although this has not always meant fragmentation),
and quite aside from the determination of market economies to
unscramble state ownership, the whole force of technology has
been working in the same direction – away from strong control
under central, and therefore heavily political, influence.

Sixth, the issue of 'the land' has come back into the debate.
For almost three decades after the Second World War, the
farming communities of Europe developed inreasingly intimate
collaboration with their national governments and later with the
European Commission. Thus, ironically, it was the traditionally
independent farmers who found themselves most closely tied
with national and supra-national power in a network of support
systems and intervention.

Now this settlement is coming apart. The cost of support,
the gross inequalities between large and small farmers, the
concentration of landholdings, the explosion of interest in
'green' issues and the expansion of light and soft industries and

enterprises in previously predominantly agricultural areas and market towns, have all combined to wreck the earlier unity of agricultural politics and interests and to open up new political battlefields for which the political parties are ill-prepared and organised. As surpluses pile up in temperate foodstuffs, and governments come under increasing pressure to curb production, we could be heading for a major farm crisis in which entirely new policy definitions will be called for so as to establish the bottom limit of rural support below which taxpayers will not be prepared to let life on the land sink.

These foodstuff surpluses are only one part of a world-wide picture of excess supply of primary commodities, including the main fuels, and therefore of falling prices. It is likely that almost all the forecasts of the past decade for the growth of demand for raw materials, for food and energy supplies will be proved wrong and have to be revised downwards drastically. The world-wide switch from energy and materials-intensive industrial processes to those based on miniature equipment and information as the 'raw material' implies a permanent shrinkage in demand for the traditional commodities, and therefore the need for a permanent change in the policies and attitudes relating to the primary producing areas, industries and committees.[1]

Seventh, the policy-makers of the late seventies were prepared for an unending struggle against inflation, the chief dragon of that decade. But the world-wide vista ahead is not primarily an inflationary one. Following the great oil shocks the economies of the advanced world have become less energy intensive, less hungry for raw materials and generally less prone to inflationary pressures. Fears of a different kind are now emerging – that disinflation will turn to deflation as decisions made in an inflationary past period, and debts incurred when it seemed safe to assume that inflation would float them off, now come to the reckoning in a quite different climate.

The collapse of crude oil prices, which has now, in the mid-eighties become so marked, is undoubtedly a most significant and visible pointer towards the new conditions which the policy-makers and economic managers now face. It can now be seen that the alleged 'scarcity' of oil, the most basic and widely traded of all the commodities, was a fiction whiich for a time

---

1. See Peter F. Drucker, *Wall Street Journal*, January 9, 1985, for some fascinating speculations on the paradox of rapid expansion in the United States and Japan combined with sustained depression in primary products.

fooled the world and distracted people from understanding much deeper underlying trends.[1]

In conventional terms of demand against available supply oil was not scarce in 1973, nor in 1979. There never was an energy crisis in the real and deep sense of overall shortage or imminent exhaustion of supplies. On the contrary, the prospect was, as remains, for an unending and growing glut of fossil fuel supplies as the entire process of industrial development moves away from its energy intensive pattern of the past and on to a miniaturised scale.

As Japanese analysts (who are proving some of the most perceptive in making sense of our new conditions) have observed, the physical resource restraint is just no longer operating in the way it did only a few years ago on the cycle of activity of the 'soft' lower-energy economy which has already emerged. We have entered a new age of growth – one which is certainly not problem-free but which presents quite novel challenges to the policy-makers, compared to those confronting us less than a decade ago.

The oil shocks of 1973 and 1979 certainly did much to obscure the picture. But they were never part of a new economic order as some suggested. Even at the time of the second oil shock, when oil prices tripled in a year, those of us who happened to be closest to it all could see that we were caught up in an unnecessary and avoidable upheaval which had little to do with the longer term trend of economic and industrial development. The so-called world energy crisis was little more than an ill-founded panic amongst major oil consumers about the continuing availability and possible political interruption of oil supplies.

So, why did the oil crisis happen at all? The immediate cause lay in the frenzied purchasing of oil, especially by Japanese and other Far Eastern buyers who were prepared to pay almost any price to get assured supplies. But behind this froth lay a long history of extraordinary policy incompetence, much of it originating in the labyrinth of American domestic politics.[2] Even at a very late stage it would have been possible to head off the 1979

1. One of the best accounts of the entire saga of the so-called energy crisis of the 1970s is to be found in Jack Anderson's *Fiasco*, (Times Books, 1983), which shows very clearly how policy incompetence and short-sightedness in the United States sowed the seeds of the two oil shocks of 1973 and 1979.
2. *Fiasco*, ibid.

price explosion, and its grim consequences for world prosperity.
Had the governments and leading oil companies of the main
oil-consuming countries taken the precaution before 1979 of
getting together to compared notes and arrange coordinated
'fire brigade' help for any market threatened with temporary
cut-off, there need have been no price explosion and no crisis.[1]

Until it was too late, these obvious steps were neglected. The
illusion of crisis was further heightened by the wild forecasts
of leading oil 'strategists'. Formidable projections went onto the
wall charts based on a wholly static analysis of events and
embodying the oldest fallacy of all, that the future would be
like the past and that oil demand would go on rising at the same
pace as it had been doing. Set alongside equally cataclysmic
prophecies about vanishing oil reserves these predictions
helped to create a picture of permanent and intensifying oil
scarcity and energy crisis.[2]

Yet all these forecasts turned out to be hopelessly wrong.
Their exponents had simply failed to grasp the wider perspective and to see that the decade of oil turbulence was an aber-
ration, and interruption in a much longer trend of change. This
trend, which was already becoming established before 1973, is
taking us far and fast away from an oil hungry world and from
the need to consume large quantities of basic raw materials.
And the pace is accelerating. It is now showing up not just in
the advanced countries, where after half a decade of industrial
growth the demand for energy and raw materials is actually
lower than at the start, but in the developing economies as
well. There the theory was that large-scale energy-intensive
technologies would first replace the primitive economic order
and then linger on, long after they had been discarded in the
richer nations. But this forecast, too, turns out to be wrong.
The poorer countries also, want their development to take them
on into the computer age.

Now that oil prices have dropped to levels which are below

1. On becoming Energy Secretary in Britain in May 1979 I sought, with my
opposite numbers in the other main oil-consuming nations, to calm the
panic-buying process, working within the forum of the Paris-based International Energy Agency. Order was restored to markets and a gradual
unwinding of prices began; but by then, of course, the initial explosion had
done its damage.
2. Professor Odell, of Rotterdam University, has impishly pointed out that
reported world reserves of oil are higher now than they were at the outset
of the oil crisis fourteen years ago.

those prevailing before the decade of upheaval began we can stand away a little and see that an intermission, a temporary fracture in the pattern of economic and social change, is over. But we do not find things as they were before. We rejoin the road again far further along, where the surrounding scenery is now quite different and where the travelling conditions have fundamentally changed.

These changes are now so pervasive that not a single day now passes without them entering into most people's daily lives and into almost every aspect of social behaviour. Within the present decade, only half over, the entire technology of industry and commerce has already been transformed almost beyond recognition. Hand in hand with this we have seen both intellectual changes of mood and a revolution in social attitudes so extensive that almost none of the assumptions about the way economies behave are now safe.

In this short period patterns of life and work have probably changed as much as they did in the previous fifty years. There is no possible way in which the policies and priorities of party politicians or of governments of the late 1970s could still be suitable in this new landscape, or still seem to connect, without drastic adaptation, with today's, let alone tomorrow's concerns.

For people and parliaments, for government and governed, for institutions and individuals the implications are direct, insistent and immense. Change or decay – that is, more than ever, the choice.

CHAPTER 2

Useless Maps

The dangers for the shapers of public policy, both in Britain and elsewhere as they march into this new country, are very great indeed. For their maps are becoming useless. They were drawn to assist the fight over other territories and by other methods.

After 1979 the chief weapon against inflation was intended to be tight control of the money supply; but turned from a commonsense broad aim into a science this has proved to be at root both a centralist and a nationalist philosophy or technique. Even if monetarism rightly questions the ability of governments to manipulate aggregate demand, it requires other powers to be available to national governments which place an equal strain on free institutions. It demands techniques for identifying and measuring, and then controlling, broad aggregates which are constantly changing shape. The electronic revolution in financial markets has made a difficult task ten times more so. 'Scientific', precision monetarism has dragged central governments into conflicts such as that with local government, where they find themselves intellectually on the wrong side. In pursuing what seemed the worthy aim of beating inflation by attempted national control of the monetary aggregates, they find themselves battering against both the deeper, and increasingly reinforced, instincts of society against centralism and against the whole trend and mood of an age in favour of greater provincialism and localism.

A further problem has been that, while the call to arms against inflation was a national one, the financial forces determining not only inflation but interest rates and the whole pace of economic activity have become even more internationalised than before. The rapid integration of world financial markets, which has greatly accelerated in the last five years, has made open economies of the British size even more exposed and vulnerable to global financial pressures than hitherto. Thus the national

crusade against inflation, for which sacrifices of interest and
principle have been demanded on all sides, is seen not only as
out of time but to be conceived on a wrong and irrelevant scale.
Jane Jacobs, in her provocation book *Cities and the Wealth of
Nations*, questions even whether nations are the right starting
points for understanding the structure of economic life at all,
or whether they ever have been. 'Nations', she writes, 'are
political and military entities, and so are blocs of nations. But
it doesn't necessarily follow from this that they are also the
basic, salient entities of economic life or that they are particularly useful for probing the mysteries of economic structure, the
reasons for the rise and decline of wealth. Indeed, the failure
of national governments and blocs of nations to force economic
life to do their bidding suggests some sort of essential
irrelevance.'

The Jacobs thought is a very damaging one for conventional
economies. Even if it was only partly valid it would still put a
question-mark over a great deal of national economic policy-
making activity. But, as we shall see in the next chapter, there
could now be forces at work in the global economy which are
turning her suspicion into a glaringly evident fact, imposing
upon us a major revision of our views about the effectiveness
of national macro-economic policy, if we are now to make any
sense at all of the world or the domestic economic scene.

Meanwhile, throughout Europe politicians have also been
driven on the defensive over the employment issue. Unable to
promise convincingly that the full employment patterns of the
past can be regained, they have also been unable to find the
right words and descriptions, and the right policy ideas, to
convey a reassuring picture of the future. The idea of a fully
occupied society which is not fully employed is, as yet, too
unfamiliar to be understood. The belief that if you are not in
full-time work you must be on the scrapheap is so deeply rooted
that it requires revolutionary persuasion to uproot it. And this
has hardly begun. But beneath this runs a much deeper problem
still – that the rhetoric and battlecries of market economics and
individual liberty, which have been used with success to mount
the assault on socialist centralism, do not provide a language
which matches the world of miniature groupings and loyalties
that is now developing in its place. Something more than the
vocabulary of market economics is needed to explain and make
sense of the new situation.

Writing in the 1830s about America, Alexis de Tocqueville described the foundations of American liberal democracy in terms which have a startling relevance and freshness for free societies in today's conditions. Peering through the surface of rugged individualism and almost caricature capitalism he saw a society founded in fact very much on co-operation, on the impulse to associate and work together and on what he called 'self interest rightly understood'.[1] It was these qualities of tempered individualism, and of instinctive readiness to come together in support of both personal and mutual interests, rather than look always to Government for protection, which gave American free society its cohesion and yet its amazing adaptability.

More recently, Western observers of post-war Japanese society have begun to illuminate for us how an intensely competitive free enterprise country like Japan nevertheless manages to be unified and extraordinarily flexible within a broad liberal democratic framework. Looking beyond what he calls the timeless generalities about 'capitalist economies' in relation to Japan Professor Ronald Dore, of the Centre for Applied Technology, has written about the 'obligational' element which enters into normal Japanese business relations and sustains the disaggregated mass of small firms and family enterprises on which the Japanese economy rests.[2] Again it is this tempered free market capitalism which both preserves and underpins Japan as a liberal democratic society which is both highly dispersed and flexible and yet also strongly unified.

Even more recently still, economists have begun to look with a new eye at a society which in the past was often dismissed as the most disorganised and anarchic of all – namely Italy. With chaotic politics, dominant unions, a huge budget deficit and haphazard administration, Italy has seemed to many the last place to look for lessons about future economic and social development. Yet it turns out that these qualities of disorganised decentralism, as manifested by the huge black economy and the spread of independent enterprise and family firms into

1. 'I am not afraid to say' wrote de Tocqueville, 'that the principle of interest rightly understood appears to me the best suited of all philosophical theories to the events of the men of our time, and that I regard it as their chief remaining security against themselves. Towards it, therefore, the minds of the moralists of our age should turn.'
   (*De la Democratie en Amerique*, 1835)
2. Hobhouse Memorial Lecture. *Goodwill and the Spirit of Market Capitalism*, 1983.

the heart of both the services and the manufacturing sectors, are precisely the ones which fit best with the electronic age. Because central government is weak, the Italian economy is flexible, highly innovative and strong. Because central bureaucracy is feeble, local enterprise, community cohesion and strong family values flourish.

Is it a coincidence that these three vigorous nations, very different in themselves, are both managing the transition to the micro-electronic epoch and the information age remarkably well? I think not. It seems to me that the message for us is fairly clear in all three cases. Modern liberal democratic societies now need more than the philosophy of free markets to sustain them and explain them. It should be no surprise that in Britain, where just the same process is going on as in Japan and America, (and to a lesser extent Italy), although a few laps behind, the counter-revolution against the dogmas and inadequacies of collectivism is itself running out of steam and relevance.

Nor is it surprising that the Conservative Government in Britain, which has nailed its colours so firmly to the mast of liberal market economics (sometimes, it seems, to the exclusion of all wider ideas and perceptions) should have appeared to lose its intellectual bearings and directions, after a period of unparalleled success in winning the political argument and keeping closely in tune with the changing public mood and outlook.

A New Policy Schedule
For the policy-makers in Britain, the key to the next period lies in three areas – first, in understanding the historic forces which are very rapidly re-defining industry, work patterns, attitudes and family and social life; second, in studying and comprehending the deeper developments going on in other liberal democratic societies, especially the Japanese but also the American, Italian and some others where the trends now being experienced here have already developed further, as have the responses to them; and third, in adapting both its policies and the way in which they are presented to connect with the new conditions. From the understanding of what is occurring, once achieved, there ought to come a new set of practical preoccupations which should govern the thinking of the intellectual leaders and provide the framework of a new appeal – perhaps

one which will have the same momentum as the arguments of
the seventies which challenged and destroyed the corporatist
and centralist ideas of an earlier period.

The new schedule should contain these questions: How is
a society to be governed which is becoming more dispersed,
and in which networks and groupings are far more localised
and pocketised, in which the old national organisations and
power-bases are much weaker and less needed? What are the
implications of these new conditions – in which economies are
changing both their shape and their behaviour – for those who
make and administer government. How is everybody to be
occupied in a society which does not require people to be all
involved in full-time labour? How is income and wealth to be
distributed, and the ownership of capital spread, in a world
in which possibly only a minority have full-time remunerated
employment and yet people live longer, are more active, have
higher expectations and want to be satisfyingly occupied
throughout life? To what extent should the state system of
redistribution of income and benefits underpin this new work
pattern and provide guaranteed income for all, whatever 'work'
they are in fact doing? How is the education system to be
expanded and reformed so as to teach societies self-reliance in
the new world of work, and so as to meet the demands from
all age groups for instructive and interesting educational and
training facilities in a wide range of skills, crafts and techniques?
And how is this enormous call on national resources to be
financed?

How do we handle the huge environmental problems of the
run-down industrial areas which must be made green again,
and of pressure on existing rural areas, of living space and of
the soaring demand coming from millions of city dwellers to
share in the countryside? How do we govern and keep alive
the cities from which most creative ideas and new industries
originate? How do we handle the land and countryside
problem, as taxpayer willingness to support European farming
weakens, as feelings mount against modern high-output agriculture and more people want a small share of the land? How
does the European Community develop if its centrepiece, the
Common Agricultural Policy, becomes impossibly expensive
and collapses? And what needs to be done on a European scale
to keep up with and compete with Asia and America? Finally,
how do we handle the world-wide consequences of the collapse

of socialist theory and the tenets of central planning? What happens to the crumbling Marx-Leninist world, to the Soviet empire in Eastern Europe and to a decentralised China?

These questions were not to the fore in 1979 in Britain, some of them had not even been raised. But, with the world transformed in the half-decade since, they are now at the heart of the policy and political debate. The politicians and shapers of policy who address them, struggle with them and listen to views upon them, will gradually assemble the maps and information necessary to meet the issues of the next decade. The leaders who ignore them and who stick to the tunes of the past will find the gulf between the world outside and their own slogans and concerns yawning impossibly wide.

PART II

The Gradual Encroachment of Ideas

'I am sure that the power of vested interests is vastly exaggerated compared with the gradual encroachment of ideas. Soon or late, it is ideas, not vested interests, which are dangerous for good or evil.'
J. M. Keynes, *The General Theory of Employment, Interest and Money*

CHAPTER 3

Centralism: The Quadruple Defeat

In the intellectual battle between capitalism and socialism there has, in the last quarter of the twentieth century, been a victory of sorts. The Western intelligentsia, who for almost a century found the social device of capitalism so displeasing, have uneasily begun to recast their views.

In fact the change of mood is evident in Asia as much as around the Atlantic seaboard and extends deep into the totalitarian world as well. In Beijing, as much as in London or Washington, in developing as well as in advanced industrial nations, views are being drastically revised about either the wisdom or the workability of central collective action by the state as the means of achieving economic and social gains, and promoting development.

The descriptive language may be different, but the trend is the same, and as we move into the second half of the 1980s it seems to be gathering force. Everywhere prices and markets are gaining respect as the mechanisms of economic and social progress. Centralism, central theories and strategies are under attack. Support for the dispersal of economic decisions on to a much wider, and much smaller, 'micro', scale is growing space, even in the most unlikely areas such as energy supply and transport, where for years past it has been assumed that large national organisations were imperative, if an efficient service was to be provided.

So in this sense the believers in salvation through the use of state power, whether Marxist or moderate, whether totalitarian or benign and trusting, like Keynes, in the rule of people 'rightly orientated in their own minds and hearts to the moral issue', have suffered a huge defeat. When Keynes wrote these words, in his famous letter to Professor Hayek praising *The Road to Serfdom*, he knew of such people. They were all around him. He knew they could govern wisely and without abuse of power; he knew, or thought he knew, that they had most of the information they required at the centre and the means of carrying their central decisions into effect. He believed, as did very many others, that his ideas could hold the middle ground between authoritarian state power and the apparent anarchy of capitalist business cycles.

So what has changed all this? The answer usually given goes as follows: Keynes's 'rightly orientated people' have long since been elbowed aside by pressures from insistent and unrestrained trade unions and by other powerful lobbies. Together these created impossible inflationary pressures in free economies which threatened to bring down the whole edifice. Various attempts have been made to intervene and control prices and wages direct, but these have all proved quite unworkable and unacceptable, except for very short periods. The value of Keynesian prescriptions, as offering the middle way between market economies and total central planning has therefore been eroded and the choice between the two systems has become starker. Meanwhile, goes the conventional explanation, the centrally planned economies have all run into enormous problems so that in these, too, people are looking with new favour on prices and markets to bail them out. Governments everywhere, it is concluded, should therefore limit themselves in the economic field to controlling the money supply and letting free markets do the rest.

Now if this is the full story, if this is the full explanation of the intellectual victory which has apparently taken place over the collectivists and the central state planners, then one would have to regard it as a very insecure victory indeed. For one thing, if classical market economics rules again, then unless there have been some other very fundamental changes as well, which we should know about and understand, there seems no reason why we should not find ourselves saddled again with all the violent cycles, the depressions, the unemployment and the general instability which gave impetus to the Keynesian alternative in the first place. For another, the arrival of monetarism at the centre of the macro-economic stage in the policy-making centres of the West has not been an unqualified success (as we shall see in later chapters of this book). Indeed, as the most enthusiastic proponents of monetary economics have had ruefully to acknowledge, the practical difficulties for national authorities of manipulating the financial aggregates, of identi-

fying, let alone controlling the various elusive concepts of
'money supply', have proved well nigh insuperable.

As I have watched at close quarters the various attempts in
Britain to implement the monetarist 'experiment', and control,
from the level of central government and the Cabinet, the
endlessly unruly aggregates, it has become evident to me that
attempts at short-term monetary management are not really a
conquering alternative to Keynesian economics at all. Indeed,
they involve very similar approaches and have similar weaknesses. To a very great extent the control of the monetary
aggregates is only one kind of national and centralist strategy,
one new set of complex functions which a central government
is somehow expected to perform, replacing another.

The situation is therefore not half so simple as the conventional account of the changing intellectual climate suggests.
Orthodox market economics are certainly having a come-back,
but it seems to me that there are also much deeper forces at
work of which it is quite essential to be aware if we are to
understand what is happening in our societies and if governments and authorities are to offer the right responses through
their policies.

'Positive knowledge', writes Bertrand de Jouvenel, 'is an
understanding of our surroundings which allows us to move
towards our goal by the best route.'[1] The resurgence of market
economics and of faith in the price mechanism are a significant
part of the new world scene but they are only a part. There
are other enormous and influential ideas as well, changes of
perception and actual physical changes in the mode of existence, which are on the march and under way and which policy-
makers neglect at their peril. To illustrate initially the nature of
some of these changes I am going to refer to the works of certain
authors and thinkers of the last two decades whose ideas have
swept us right on past the debates between Keynesians and
monetarists and which have challenged some of the deepest
foundations upon which economics is based. They are not the
only ones to have shaken orthodoxy but their thinking, which
crystallises the views of many other writers as well, comes over
with exceptional clarity and force.

In 1973 R. F. Schumacher's *Small is Beautiful* was published

---

1. From *Capitalism and the Historians*, edited by F. A. Hayek, Routledge and
Kegan Paul Ltd., 1954.

in London.[1] Schumacher, who had worked for the National
Coal Board, had a message which blasted a hole with torpedo-
like force in the tenets of collectivism and centralism, and in
the entire style of thinking and policy making which treated
society as a mass, a conglomeration of aggregates to be
influenced and managed by big government and big central
institutions. Both ideas and technology, he explained to a
surprised world, were taking us rapidly away from large-scale
organisation as the essential engine of prosperity and well-
being, and from large-scale, or 'macro' policy making generally.
Noting that economics had obviously failed so far to settle down
as a modest occupation similar to dentistry, as Keynes hoped
it would,[2] Schumacher ridiculed the growing impotence of
national economic policies, even though they seemed to absorb
almost the entire attentions of governments. Organisation on a
large scale, he argued, with its strutting undertones of giantism,
was becoming increasingly inappropriate and ineffective, partly
because of much greater mobility across frontiers but even more
so because national economic viability was really a non-ques-
tion. 'There is no such thing' he declared 'as the viability of
states or of nations, there is only the problem of viability of
people.'[3] What Schumacher was saying tended to be seized
upon by environmentalists and ecologists to confirm their fears
about industrial concentration, whether socialist or capitalist,
and his book certainly provided ammunition for these causes.
But it has always seemed to me that his message for the macro-
economists, with their national aggregates, their levers to
control demand or credit or the national money supply, or
consumption or employment or the price level, was just as
telling. There, too, it might be time to change the emphasis and
begin to focus on smaller scale issues and problems.

Another writer, who has also driven a coach and horses
through the science and practice of macro-economics is Jane
Jacobs, whose successive books on the real forces that create
wealth, markets and jobs have begun to make the orthodox and
mainstream economists, Keynesian and monetarist, worriedly
re-examine some of their assumptions. Jacobs, whose works are
less well known in Europe than in America, points out that the
science of macro-economics is now a shambles. The stagflation

1. Blond & Briggs.
2. J. M. Keynes, Collected writings, Vol. II, p. 332.
3. *Small is Beautiful*, chapter 5.

(the combination of rising prices and high unemployment) that ought not to exist in theory, does exist. Attempts to grapple with it either by Keynessan techniques of trade-off between inflation and unemployment, or by efforts to identify and then somehow tighten down elusive concepts like the national money supply, have produced distressingly and puzzlingly poor results. She believes, like Schumacher, that the heart of the problem is the erroneous idea that econommes really exist at all as national blocks of activity. Her persuasive thesis is that to understand why peoples and their surroundings prosper, why economies grow or decline, one should look at cities and their regions, not at nations. It iscities and all the rich, or not so rich, patterns of economic activity within them which are unique, she maintains, in shaping both their own hinterlands and other regions with which they do business.

We do not need to go all the way with the fascinating Jacobs analysis to see that her message for national economic policy-makers is a deeply unsettling one. Nations obviously exist as sovereign entities, with strong political and military expression. No one doubts that. But is there really anything approximating to a national economy, a single mass with a common behaviour pattern responding to single central acts of economic policy? It is not a question to which Adam Smith gave much attention, starting as he did in the very first sentence of *The Wealth of Nations* by taking the idea of the Gross National Product for granted.[1] But it must certainly be a question that crosses the mind of the struggling central economic policy-maker today as he sees the financial indicators and aggregates melt away into an international mish-mash of electronic money, or dissolve into a patchwork of local economic activities which may be responding in quite different and even contradictory ways to the same single national policy measure.

There is another school of thought which starts from the same point – the declining effectiveness of macro-economic policy – but takes us in a rather different direction. The proponents of this school ask why national governments are now failing so conspicuously to 'deliver' mass full-employment in the way that

1. See page 1 of *The Wealth of Nations*. 'The annual labour of every nation is the fund which originally supplies it with all the necessaries and conveniences of life which it annually consumes, and which consists always either in the immediate produce of that labour, or in what is purchased with that produce from other nations.'

they formerly seemed able to do. They conclude that in the new industrial landscape we now inhabit, patterns of work, attitudes to work and types of work have already developed which can no longer be tidily manoeuvred by central bureaucratic action, indeed can no longer even be documented and moulded into the neat aggregates which central economic planners like to use as their building blocs.

Two eloquent authors of recent books on this new work pattern, and its huge implications for national economic policy-makers (as well as for the current political debate), are Charles Handy (*The Future of Work*) and James Robertson (with his similarly titled *Future Work*). We shall have much more to say on their analyses and their implications in Section 4 of this volume. In the meantime it should be emphasised that neither book is a work of futurology. Both are concerned with the pattern of practice of work here and now in Britain, in the late 1980s. Both suggest that conventional patterns of paid employment are being superseded by much more flexible and personal work arrangements for both men and women and that the great central institutions of power, such as the nationally organised unions, and the nationally designed policies in support of a society of employees, are increasingly ineffectual and inappropriate to real everyday life and work.

All these, and many other, studies suggest very strongly that the language and modes of thought in which national governments have been accustomed to depict their policies and plans will no longer really do. We are passing through a period of enormous change in social attitude and behaviour, involving a major retreat from centralism with high implications for public policy. But, aside from changing economic views and changing habits, the world being buffeted by other even more powerful forces. The new factor is a technology so vast, so pervasive and so revolutionary that it leaves no part of life, or word, or government untouched. What needs to be added to the picture of which we have so far only sketched the outlines, is an appreciation not just of the growth of this even greater force, but of the fact that it is working in exactly the same direction. The enormous pressures latent in micro-technology are giving an explosive push towards dispersal, fragmentation and decentralisation in society, striking a further devastating blow at central and national influence and bureaucratic organisation, and changing the way economies behave.

Once we start exploring the impact of cheap and widespread computer power and of the information revolution on central government policy (and again this is a process already well under way), and once all the pressures from this direction are added to the changes already long identified by Schumacher, Jacobs, Handy and many others, we will then, and only then begin to get a sense of the immense defeat of centralism in society which is being inflicted and the size and nature of the victory that is being gained by the new ideas which are now encroaching from several angles on conventional thinking. It is this quite amazing change, the quite suddenly accelerating decline in the capacities of central administrations to find out, to organise or to act in matters of economic and social behaviour, combined with the realisation that such scale and size is anyway being made obsolete by new, miniaturised electronic technology, as well as being hopelessly cumbersome and insensitive, that the mind attuned to the beneficent power of big government, and to macro-economics generally, finds it almost impossibly hard to accept.

In effect, we are seeing a quadruple defeat of centralism. Market forces are proving superior to state planning: faith in national economic aggregates and their manipulation is declining; social attitudes towards work and central control and provision are being revolutionised: micro-electronics are opening up a new world of dispersed economic decisions and dispersed power which, as we shall see, even the most steel-fisted tyrannies cannot resist. We need to understand the anatomy of these defeats and we need to learn and understand the true nature of the apparent victory over the centrists, the aggregatists, the opponents of free markets and the collectivists which has taken place. Not to do so is to run the risk both of repeating great mistakes and losing great opportunities.

CHAPTER 4

The Aggregates Let Everyone Down

Official statistics have become wildly inaccurate. The Central Statistical Office is still revising its measurements of the rate of growth of national output of four or five years back. For the late seventies its original growth figures now appear to have been up to one hundred per cent out and its figures for the much larger figure of national product itself out more than once by at least seven per cent.

Export figures invariably have to be substantially revised. Measurements of total national investment turn out to be ten per cent too small. Huge financial aggregates like sterling M3 – the supposed measure of the broad stock of money – turn out to be so variable and vague, and so much under the influence both of global trends and of new monetary technology in an increasingly deregulated financial system that they are discarded as useful indicators. Even narrower measurements which attempt to define actual money in use, within national boundaries are proving hopelessly unreliable indicators.

What is going on? The answer is that no one is very sure. The world of macro-economics is in a state of unparalleled confusion as the building blocs on which much of it was founded, the so-called economic and financial aggregates, turn out to be made of sand.

Three decades ago at Cambridge Nicholas Kaldor, the dazzling disciple of Keynes, was using his powerful mind to make nonsense of the aggregate concepts upon which the much more timid monetarism then being practised by the British Government was based. Long before the advent of electronic money he was insisting that unmeasurable, indeed largely unknown but very frequent variations in the velocity of money, the speed at which measurable money was moved from one use to another, made attempts to control the actual money supply futile, especially attempts to make small and fine changes in something so amorphous and elastic.[1]

But of course the intellectual weapons that Kaldor used against the policy mixture of the day and the aggregates on which it rested, could be, and have been, used with just as great effect against the aggregate foundations of Keynesian analysis itself. Investment, consumption, final demand, the employment level, the level of real wage rates – all these were the essentials from which Keynesian macro-economics had to start. But if they, too, are all so unreliable that they do not measure what is really happening, on what do the economic policy-makers rest their broad 'macro' plans? What if the safe official world of Blue Books and Annual Abstracts of Statistics, of banking figures, of output by industrial sector all begins to become detached from the real economy and the real structure of industry and work?

But of course, it will be said, there must be some absolutely definite figures like, for example, the numbers who are registered unemployed and drawing unemployment benefit. But here, too, the keepers of the statistics in the Department of Employment have found that nothing is what it seems by a very long way. It turns out that between a quarter and a third of those registered in Britain are not actively seeking work. Noone knows whether they are 'unemployed' or not.[2] It also appear that there may be another million or so who do feel 'unemployed' but have not bothered to register, which explains why public debate even using the conventional definitions covers a range of figures from 1½ million to five million unemployed in Britain.[3]

These are not minor statistical quibbles. The official figures showing mass unemployment were really the starting point, the foundation for the whole Keynesian argument that central government should 'do something', indeed the starting point for modern macro-economic thinking. Yet the foundations seem to be dissolving. The official figure is becoming a less and less adequate indicator of actual employment levels and to be unable to pick up and reflect the new patterns of work emerging all through society.

1. See *Essays on Economic Policy* by Nicholas Kaldor, Duckworth, 1964.
2. Pointed out by Lord Young, the Employment Secretary, in an article in *The Times*, 5.10.85.
3. See *Employment Gazette*, October 1985.

In fact there seem to be signs, in many of the advanced economies, that work and economic activity, far from becoming better documented and recorded in the computer age, are becoming much more difficult to measure in a useful way. This is not surprising. Economies that are becoming much more dispersed, with many more 'micro' enterprises, with much more work being done from home and by increasing numbers of people who are partly and fully self-employed, are actually becoming less visible and much less easy to regiment, although of course much more flexible and adaptable.

Later on we shall see how the Japanese have noted these new qualities in their own economic structure and are beginning to develop a coherent approach to, and policies for, the new conditions they observe. But we do not need to go to Asia to find other very striking examples of economies becoming decreasingly visible and responsive to central government economic policy, yet increasingly adaptive and sufficient.

In 1982 Charles Sabel, of the Massachusetts Institute of Technology, undertook a study of the amazing industrial vitality of Northern Italy.[1] Sabel marvelled at the enormous range of tiny enterprises he found there, not just in services but in many forms of manufacturing, all achieving economies of scale which conventional thinking associates only with giant organisations. He observed the ease of breakaway and start-up by new small firms, the efficiency, the use of high and miniaturised technology, and concluded that he was seeing first signs of 'an epochal redefinition of markets, technologies and industrial hierarchies'.[2]

The phenomenon Sabel noted was all taking place inside a society in which the hand of central government, and the burden of central economic policy, rested very lightly indeed. Not only does the local commune in Italy have a quite extraordinary degree of influence on local economic activity, but the Italian central government operates a strategic economic and financial policy which by recent British policy-making standards is dangerously relaxed. A huge government borrowing requirement, monetary laxity and a detached attitude to wage settlements provide a context in which inflation is nevertheless falling, as it is throughout the planet, with one or two Latin

1. 'Italy; High Technology Cottage Industry.' *Transatlantic Perspectives* 1982. Quoted by Jane Jacobs, page 40.
2. Ibid.

American exceptions. Productivity is soaring and wealth being created on a triumphant scale (although much of it is then siphoned off into a notably non-performing southern Italian economy).

The Italian example reinforces usefully two messages. The first of these is that technology and miniaturisation are making nonsense of the arguments about the need for industrial scale, for big aggregated industrial enterprises. The second message seems to be that central government economic policies are not very important. If they were, then Northern Italy would be in ruins, with economists shaking their heads over its poor performance and blaming it on the lack of clear central strategies and strong national economic direction from Rome.

There is also a third influence we should take into account in seeing how the tide has turned against aggregatism. This is the political revulsion against the sort of policy-making which aggregatism seems to require and the sorts of groups and institutions in whose hands it places power. If one believes, for example, that there is a definable category called 'the workers' then the claim of the trade union movement to speak for this entity through its General Council seems plausible. If one assumes that British Industry is merely an agglomeration of large and medium-sized firms which employ people, then it seems natural that the Confederation of British Industry should speak for that, too.

During the 1970s in Britain, when a great deal of public policy seemed to be settled between these impressive corporate bodies, often over the head of Parliament, a considerable antagonism grew up to what was dubbed 'consensus government'. At the start the word 'consensus' had sounded good and all-embracing, an idea which seemed to involve everybody. Lyndon Johnson was very fond of it. He saw it as the foundation idea on which to build his plan for 'The Great Society'.

But as the decade proceeded, some rather awkward doubts began to intrude. Did the 'consensus' partners really embrace 'everybody'? What about the millions who were not trade unionists (quite aside from the millions who were but played no very active part)? And what about the millions of people who were not working in CBI member firms, or who were not even working in recognisable firms at all?

As long as these were the doubts of a marginal minority they could be brushed aside. But what the politics of the 1970s in

Britain revealed was that the margin was beginning to become as wide as the print on the page. The 'aggregate' categories whose spokesmen were so confidently laying down national policy guidelines and explaining how the economy should be run simply left too many people in the real world out of account. When it also became clear that the great trade union army was a force of generals without troops, or at any rate without obedient troops, and that it could not deliver promised patterns of behaviour, all political confidence in the consensus system evaporated.

The policy vacuum that this débâcle left was one which was promptly filled by the monetarists. But in their enthusiasm to man the breach the new theorists seem to have ignored the real lessons of their victory. It is not just Keynesian aggregatism which is being discredited, but the whole science of macroeconomics. This is because both attitudes and technology are working on each other to erode and reject the entire style of mass and 'block' thinking about economic life from which the macro-economists start. So we are not, as some seem to have thought, just dealing with a return to fashion of market economics – a fashion which, like others could easily pass.

The forces dictating change are now making economies literally less controllable. They are also weakening the demand that there should be, or need be, such control from the centre. Central control is becoming less necessary and less efficient, while more personal and local and dispersed control is becoming comfortable and, as we shall see in the next section of this book, much more practicable. In this changing context national monetary policy, which in some sense relies as much as Keynesianism on central government omniscience about a range of ill-defined concepts, was always likely to be fraught with difficulties and surprises, and this has indisputably proved to be the case. Crumbling aggregates have undermined not just Keynesian prescriptions. They have made macro-economists of all schools wonder about the basic assumptions on which their ideas are based.

The monetarist theory that an increase in the supply of money (if that can be measured) against a fixed supply of goods (if goods can be measured) reduces the value of money itself must, in the abstract, be correct. But the new centrists in monetary garb have been quite unable to answer doubts as to whether monetary discipline is in practice possible, whether the supply of money – even narrow, 'transactions' money – can be defined, let alone controlled and whether the indicators of apparent change in the monetary aggregates are remotely reliable.

By the autumn of 1985 the official policy world in Britain was beginning to recongise ruefully what more cautious monetarists had been warning about since the beginning of the decade, namely, that the monetary aggregates were being shot to pieces by computerised banking, by far more sensitive and rapid movements of funds in and out of different financial instruments, and by the maddening perversity of the public in switching their funds around so as to seek the best rate of return (thus inflating sterling M3 for example out of all meaning).

In this book *Wealth and Poverty*, George Gilder reaches this conclusion: 'Like aggregate demand, the money supply is an essentially mathematical concept that means less than it seems.'[1] And like such concepts, he might have added, it depends even for its mathematical worth on flows of information to the central co-ordinating bureaucracy which might at one time have been clear controllable streams but which have now swollen to muddy uncontrollable torrents from a thousand sources. Widely dispersed and geometrically expanded information handling and trading has washed out and dissolved the mysteries of macro-economics just as surely as the spread of printing technology took power and mystery from the monasteries after Gutenberg had set up his presses at Mainz.

These trends towards uncontrollability are evident in seats of central government almost everywhere in the advanced world. They call into question the whole basis of macro-economic thinking as we shall see in later chapters. But for the smaller economies like the British, in contrast to the American continental bloc, the problems of control are being still further compounded by another powerful and spreading influence. This is the process by which information technology has begun to push capital markets together, squash global financial transactions into one vast network and internationalise finance at a speed and in a way which makes nonsense of attempts at national policy control.

Capital flows now dwarf trade flows in determining exchange rates. Vast sums can now be transferred round the electronic circuit of world financial centres with unbelievable swiftness.

1. George Gilder *Wealth and Poverty* page 191 (Buchan & Enright) 1982.

In the absence of elaborate capital controls at national frontiers, which are probably now unenforceable except in the completely closed Communist economies (and may be breaking down even in these), huge sums of cash or near-money can swirl into the national system overnight and swirl out again, leaving behind a pile of statistical debris for central bankers to sort through. For free economies, the information explosion, and the amazing expansion of instant and continuous intercontinental communications, have made domestic monetary policy almost an irrelevance – a point to which we return in Chapter V. The citizen with full connection to the information network from his home or his office can now stretch, as it were, both beyond and beneath his national masters. He or she can now both receive, reciprocate and instruct with a speed and detail and on a scale which bypasses national administration, and their frontiers, and which connects up instantly with the people at the end of the street.

The decline of faith in economic aggregatism, and the decline in the conceptual and technical reliability of those aggregates, whether used by Keynesians or monetarists, by dedicated central planners or mild formulators of 'indicative' national industrial strategies, is a matter of the utmost significance not just for economic policy advisers and makers but for the whole structure of the economy and the whole range of economic and social policy. We may conclude that the behaviour of advanced economies is changing, that detailed relationships within these economies are altering, and therefore the response to given sets of measures and given policy approaches is also changing, and doing so very fast and on a very large scale.

This is not just a hypothesis, a quick gathering of straws in the wind to make up one of several possible tableaux of tomorrow, while the practical men get on with today's problems. The landscape has already changed. The new patterns of behaviour can already be discerned. The need is for understanding and coherent explanations of what appears to be happening and for attitudes and approaches at the level of both central and local government which fit the new landscape scene, rather than ignore it or cut across it.

Japan is a society in which that need seems to be getting some positive and creative recognition in intellectual circles. That makes Japan not just a nation of amazing innovative and adaptive technological power but also a country which is giving the most profound thought to the forces at work at a most minute level within it. From some of the new intellectual concepts which the Japanese are developing which take us away on from the present macro-economic policy debate in Western Europe, and open up new terrain, we have much to learn. In the next chapter we have a first look at some of them.

CHAPTER 5

Introducing Softnomics

The ugly word 'softnomics' has been dreamt up by Japanese thinkers to describe the study and behaviour of the soft, dispersed sort of economy which is replacing the old industrial structure in advanced countries. The concept is useful because it tackles the conventional thinking of economists, Keynesian and monetarists, head-on. The premises behind it are first that economies no longer behave in the familiar cyclical way dictated by traditional capital-intensive and energy-intensive industry, and second, that information in the advanced economies about what is really happening in work and business is getting both more voluminous and less reliable at the same time.

The observation of the softnomics school is that with the spread of micro-electronics and cheap personal computers, opportunities are opening up for an infinitely greater decentralisation of enterprise. This involves many more, and more dispersed decision points, to the extent where their range and number makes keeping track of them impossible. Put another way, the soft economy ceases to have commanding heights and therefore ceases to respond to policies which attempt to command those heights. The centre grows weaker as power and knowledge spread outwards on the wings of modern information circuits and powerful data handling tools.

The Japanese thinkers have sought to define the development of the soft economy statistically, as well as in terms of its novel behaviour. They argue that it is measured by the rising ratio of fixed investment in non-manufacturing industries to investments in the 'hard' industries such as steel, automobiles, heavy engineering, ship-building. They also measure the 'softnomics' characteristic by the rise in the ratio of non-physical 'raw material', such as information, research on knowledge-based products, to total raw material input costs.[1]

This is perhaps contradictory in that the kind of society they are discussing is one in which, by definition, precise central knowledge which can be neatly aggregated and parcelled does not exist. But it serves as a broad definition of what is meant.

The softnomics idea is also interesting for what it says about the changing nature of commercial transactions between individuals and groups. Are the simple verities of marketplace economics, and of arms-length dealings, sufficient to describe the way people respond to economic signals and do business with each other in its new environment? The students of the soft economy think not. Their basic contention is that in a more diffused society something more than purely economic calculation begins to enter into contracts and business deals. Self-interest may be the driving force, but it is a tempered kind of self-interest. People and enterprises desire the survival of each other as economies become more flexible and less dominated by giant organisations; business relationships become less coldly institutional again, more personal and more influenced by non-economic considerations such as keeping the other fellow in business, maintaining some kind of job and status for each worker or ensuring that enough younger people are trained.

The word 'again' is relevant because in some ways what is being described here is in line with the kind of pattern based on family and inter-family businesses, and very local business dealings which supposedly existed before urbanisation and the industrial revolution had their full impact on nineteenth century society. Indeed, we are back here with the quality de Tocqueville was trying to capture when he described American economic motives in the 1830s as being driven by 'self-interest rightly understood', in contrast to the usual picture of naked individualism. Instead he painted a picture of a society based far more on associations, communities and familities and far less on classic individualism than any of the usual pastiches of American economic life offered by European observers.

The de Tocqueville insight is of the utmost significance in today's context. It seems to coincide almost precisely with the

1. These concepts have been developed in particular by Professor Royama at Osaka University. They are also reflected in official Japanese statements. See, for example, the 1985 Ministry of Finance White Paper 'Issues for a New Round of Growth'.

sort of attitudes which the Japanese 'softnomics' analysts and thinkers are trying to describe one hundred and fifty years later at the very frontiers of high technology and the information revolution. The idea of 'self interest rightly understood' as the binding force keeping a society together is something alien to the thinking of industrialised Europeans, despite its early identification by the French writer. It cannot be fitted into the theories of state power or the philosophies of individualism to which European political debate is reduced. It implies that the choice for a society is not polarised. It is not a question of *either* paternalism and the collectivist state, with consequent loss of freedom, *or* individual freedom and rights, with consequent loss of order. There is a pattern of behaviour, mutually supportive but also self-reliant, which lies in between, which gives coherence and unity to the atoms of society and which is not merely possible, but is *normal*.

In other words, the right lesson to draw from de Tocqueville, as well as from analysis of changing Japanese society under the impact of information technology, is that the stereotype of economic man was, and is now more than ever, something of a parody. The Benthamite preoccupation with individual welfare can therefore perhaps be better understood as a reaction against the collectivist state despotism of earlier European periods than as a confident new philosophy in its own right. If the de Tocqueville message is valid then the opposite to state control never has been ruthless individualism and the market economy has never really rested on millions of supposedly purely economic decisions. Other motives are also universally at work. Mention has already been made of the obligational element in Japanese society, a quality which reflects a Japanese businessman's recognition of the other party's status, dignity and right to exist and trade when making business contracts.

Professor Dore does not see this enlightenment, if that is the right word, as being a sort of offshoot of philanthropy. It is more subtle than that. He speaks of high-trust relationships as being preferred to openly adversarial bargaining. Writing particularly of labour markets and agreements to hire, he argues that 'the contract is seen, in fact, less as any kind of bilateral bargain, than as an act of admission to an enterprise community, wherein benevolence, goodwill and sincerity are explicitly expected to temper the pursuit of self interest.'[1]

Nothing of this different kind of attitude shows up in the conventional accounts or the national income and output statistics, because these conventional indications do not measure quality as a solid well-being. Yet in the Japanese case the consequences do emerge in a highly significant way – namely in the plentiful supply of work apparently available for about all who want it. Whether one looks at small business or large, family enterprises, part-time work or thinly disguised employment, especially evident in the retail trade, the picture is the same and the results are the same. Japan enjoys an almost uniquely low level of visibly unemployed and a uniquely high capacity to absorb people of all intelligence levels into occupations that at least *seem* useful and give some minimum level of dignity to the individual.

This is an ideal which the British and other European economies fully shared until only the other day. It was called the commitment to full employment – universal job provision. This was the way in which our version of the same social obligation was expressed.

But from there things have developed in a fundamentally different way. In the Western case it was left to the Government and the state to do the expressing. People could put these demanding questions of duty and obligation in business and trade safely out of their minds because 'they' the government were the ones supposed to be shouldering the social task of ensuring that everyone who so wished was usefully employed in some function or other.

The weakness in the Western situation when Government finds itself no longer able to deliver on the employment front is obvious and central. A huge vacuum of both understanding and action opens up. People are simply not acclimatised to the idea of taking up, either on a community or personal level, responsibility for actions which it was always assumed the Central Government would perform by some macro-economic policy magic. Once this assumption is challenged there can surely be no question but that we pass through a doorway into an entirely new landscape of ideas and policies.

---

1. Referred to by Professor Ronald Dore in his *Studies in the Japanese Textile Industry*.

The central claim and purposes of modern 'macro' or large scale economics has been that national governments can, by operating at these general economic levels, do something towards creating a society which is fully employed. Suppose then, first that while people certainly want to work they no longer all want to have employee status, so that the very meaning of full employment begins to change radically. And suppose, second, that the new alternative pattern which people really do much prefer is more likely to come from attacking the problems of wages and work at its roots, at the micro-economic level, than by pushing and pulling the levels of the macro-economy at central government level. If these two suppositions can be proved to have substance, then they tear the heart out of macro-economic thinking and present central policy-makers with completely new challenges. Let us see where the possibilities take us.

CHAPTER 6

A Better Behaviour Pattern

The classical economists recognised the existence of business cycles but they offered no solution to them. Alfred Marshall conceded that there could be 'a crisis of confidence', others, like Mill, had recognised that equilibrium could be temporarily upset and markets deranged.

All this was swept aside by the hideous reality of the Great Depression and the claims of the new macro-economists that central Governments could take remedial action. The propositions of the great Professor Pigou, who had been Keynes's teacher, that wage adjustments must in due course, if not instantaneously, restore employment, were aggressively attacked by both Keynes himself and his followers.

There were much better answers to hand, it was claimed. Fiscal and monetary policy, manipulated and fine-tuned by the state authorities, could simply cut out all this nonsense about wage adjustment. The spotlight swung away from the micro-economy towards the majestic ramparts of macro-economic strategy. That is where the solutions would be found.

Despite the monetarist counter-revolution of recent years, that is where the prevailing wisdom rests. Something called full employment can be restored. The cry that the central Government must 'do something' to bring this about has been, and continues to be the raw material of books, speeches and articles about the unemployment question. For most of the authors of these works and views there continues to be very little doubt about the matter. Whatever may be happening in other societies, whatever the puzzling and contradictory signs coming from the labour market that it is no longer organised in the traditional way, it is from the central state, goes the claim, that the necessary moves must come to get everyone into some kind of employed work. The central government, says this view loud and clear, is the purveyor of dignity and status for each individual, the corporate body with the power and responsibility to arrange full employment, which is held to be the only valid form of work. Along with this goes the assumption that it is well within the capacity of modern states to deliver, that national governments know enough at the centre about supply and demand in the labour market to press the right switches and fill the gap torn in our society by unemployment and the instabilities of the business cycle.

In his lucid volume *Britain Can Work*, Ian Gilmour puts the point about as clearly as anyone can. 'Without measures to expand aggregate demand,' he declares, 'unemployment will go on rising indefinitely.' 'The state', he continues, 'has a duty to act. . . There must therefore be expansion and there must be special measures to reduce unemployment.' He is sure that the Treasury could do something if only it was not in the grip of such perverse policies, but 'it prefers to spend £15 billion to pay people to do nothing rather than act to make the payment of such a sum unnecessary'.

Gilmour speaks for a large body of opinion which continues to believe absolutely in the power of macro-economics to get things done, and therefore in the existence of the means through which this power can be exercised. The question of whether this power, or those means, do in fact still exist in quite the form which conventional aggregatist economics assumes, does not really enter the argument. It is assumed from the outset. So is the nature of the unemployment which macro-policy is meant to cure. So is the character of the labour market, and so are people's motives, attitudes to work and ways of organising their lives. Employment is the thing.

As we shall see in Part V of this book, all these assumptions are in practice becoming very unsafe indeed. We may actually already be in a world where they are invalid. But that is not the concern of the macro-economic devotees nor has it got anything to do with the Keynesian analysis or prescription.

Later on in *Britain Can Work* Ian Gilmour's views become a bit more qualified about what in fact can be done by individual governments. 'There is a limit,' he says, 'to what we can do acting by ourselves . . . It is a European problem and almost a world-wide one. Certainly, no country can solve it on its own.' Nevertheless, the central message is clear and confident. It is that it is up to the national government to act. The state must intervene. Economic and financial aggregates exist which can and must be manoeuvred so as to create a state of full-employment. The levers are there; they work, they must be operated.

But supposing they do not work? What if the central government in an economy like Britain's is much less well-equipped with the necessary knowledge, information and weapons to conduct a successful macro-economic strategy than has been assumed ever since Keynes? And suppose, too, that full-employment in the broad sense of providing most people, the vast majority in fact, with a full-time paid job as someone else's employee – a 'proper job' – is no longer what people need and want? What then?

The thought does not yet seem to have dented the thinking of the enthusiasts for state action in this field, that in the one country where registered unemployment has been maintained at staggeringly low levels through all the ups and downs of recent decades, and where it is showing no real signs of emerging despite immensely rapid technological progress – namely Japan – the whole emphasis has been not on more and more central state intervention but on less. Japanese society may well have great cohesion and a strong sense of common aims and purposes. But that seems to go not with ever more embracing state activities but with less. The fierce Japanese belief is in small, not large government, and this is reflected in lower levels of taxation and a lower share of government spending in the gross national product, as well as in a rising intellectual interest in the very different behaviour of a more dispersed, 'soft' economy which we touched on in the last chapter.

There is also another feature buried in the Japanese system which the post-Keynesians ought to examine in reassessing their pre-occupation with macro-economic 'solutions'. Obviously, the Japanese labour market is 'different' in very many ways from the labour scene in Britain or elsewhere in Europe. But there is one contrast with British practice which stands out above all. Throughout almost the entire employed sector remuneration is organised in a way which by-passes the simple wage system. All pay, which tends anyway to be on a monthly salary basis for all grades, rather than in the form of an hourly wage, is divided into component parts. One part is the traditional fixed-rate wage. The other part is the bonus which is really a profit-share and which varies with the firm's and the individual's performance. Typically this second part is about a quarter of the total package and is paid twice a year.

The essential point to understand about this bonus element is that it is not a wage and does not perform the same economic role as a wage. First, because it is not part of the fixed wage system it does not necessarily come into a firm's thinking when it takes on new workers. New recruits are hired at the basic, familiar wage, which is by definition lower than likely total remuneration. The incentive to take on new workers is correspondingly increased. Thus the problem at the centre of Keynesian concern, that wages were inflexible downwards, whatever the classical economists said, and that macro-economic devices offered the only answer, is at once significantly reduced.

Second, the existence of this element, which is related both psychologically and in practice to the profit performance of the enterprise, and to the world of capital, investment and savings rather than of income and pay, has a crucial influence on the entire Japanese economic and financial culture. Japan has the characteristics of what is called a share economy. That is to say, the majority rather than a minority, are involved with non-wage forms of family and personal finance, whether through the bonus system sketched here or through actual stock ownership or through the colossally extended pattern of small and family businesses which form the underbed of the entire Japanese economic structure. Because people think of themselves as capital owners as well as wage earners they think and begin to act differently. And it is not very surprising that they do. Connection to the economic society through more than the thin thread of a weekly or hourly wage is bound to transform attitudes, and clearly has in Japan. A society in which the vast majority are accustomed to handling capital sums rather than weekly wage packets seems bound to be more responsible, have a greater sense both of belonging to a large community and of obligations to that community, and generally to think a little further ahead, than a society which knows nothing of capital, indeed fears it as a hostile force, and lives only for wages.

Many people will argue that Japan is so different from Britain that this example of Japanese behaviour means nothing in the British context. Yet surely on the contrary, there is a lesson here of the utmost significance for British policy. For if such enormous strides towards achieving the goal of a fully-occupied society can be taken by means of changes in the detailed relationships at the level of the firm, the micro-economic level, ought not the embattled 'macro' experts, who have so notably failed to produce the results for which they hoped and who have evidently lost their way, to be looking in these new directions for some better way forward? Ought not micro-economics in fact come to the rescue of the bewildered macro-economic engineers? Ought it not to point us both toward the familiar economic goals of full-employment (of some kind) and of greater economic stability, and to the social goals of greater responsibility, better care for the weak, less poverty, less crime and a generally fuller and more satisfying life for all?

Hitherto, the riposte to this sort of thinking has been familiar. It is that this is idealism and fantasy. The real world is one of unstable markets, ruthless individualism with the weakest to the wall. That is why Governments must step in and take command of sufficient resources to provide the stability and the occupations for all which competitive capitalism will not provide.

Yet, quite aside from de Tocqueville's insights into the way people really behaved long ago in young America, which seem flatly to contradict this, the Japanese example of today must make us ask whether the classical paternalist model of social behaviour which may or may not have been valid at the height of the industrial revolution, still makes sense now in wholly changed industrial and work conditions. Could it be that nowadays, if people and groups of people are left more to their own devices, their patterns of economic and social behaviour, and therefore the behaviour of the entire system of which they are the component parts, will act after all in a steadying and involving sort of way? Could this new kind of laissez faire be a stabilising force? Could there be everywhere in advanced societies, and not just in the Japanese 'special case', a growing sense of duty and obligation ready to be reinstated in people's behaviour which might go far towards 'solving' the unemployment problem in a way that state action has failed so notably to do, and failed on a world-wide scale?

If there really are such motives and forces, then how are they to be activated and drawn out? Not, clearly, by macro-economic lever-pulling, whether of the Keynesian or monetarist variety. And not by centrally organised strategies for restoring patterns of full employment that simply do not fit in with either the needs of industry today or the wants of individual people and families, which correspond neither with the demand side nor the supply side of the revolutionised labour market now developing. If the world is not at all as Marx or Keynes saw it, if the smaller components of society, far below the level of the national policy-constructors, really are in a stronger position to attain widely sought social goals than their central government masters, then we are truly in a revolutionary position.

The comparison which critics will draw is with nineteenth century laissez faire liberalism, with leaving the system, warts and all, to look after itself. But that is to miss the main point. What we may now have is a world which has passed through the necessary paternalist phases to which Keynesianism gave ultimate and brilliant expression and which, thanks to staggering technological advance, can now operate on a far more deregulated, less organised basis again.

My own belief is that we have reached well into this stage and later chapters will try and show this to be so in some detail. But the policy-makers have to be converted as well. It has to be convincingly shown not just that new conditions are emerging in our societies but that many widely-held assumptions embedded in the current policy schedule are no longer valid and no longer connect with real life. There will have to be the cutting of some familiar ties. In the next and last chapter in this part of the book, which has been concerned with the encroachment of new ideas, we will have a closer look at these ties and attempt to understand what it was, and still is, that those who cling to them so tenaciously, who believe so sincerely in central manipulation of the aggregates and in state-devised strategies, have been trying to achieve. We will show that their most cherished goals can almost certainly now be secured in better and different ways.

CHAPTER 7

Why Did it all Last so Long?

What were the dilemmas and the problems which the macro-economists thought they could solve through the agency of national governments?

In the 1930s the first answer to that question would have been that Keynes could save us from Marx. Capitalism was certainly in crisis, the phenomenon of unemployment was real, evident and harsh and here was a new way on offer of restoring stability which was not authoritarian, not even strongly socialist, and which could head off collapse. This was the Keynesian godsend – a state-inspired means of proving Marxian economics historically and fundamentally wrong. The central Marxian message was chillingly clear. There would be a collapse of purchasing power, a deadly deficiency of demand inside each national economy (note that Marx, like Adam Smith, thought and argued as though national economies were valid and identifiable entities). It was this that would lead to the falling rate of profit, the collapse of capitalism into barbarism and to bloody revolution.

It was therefore a matter of the utmost urgency to establish that this fatal deficiency could be remedied and sufficient purchasing power generated to put the national economy back on its feet. Arguments about the misallocation of resources, about the need to make markets work and other contentions, which would today be described as 'supply-side' concerns, were swept to the winds. As we have seen, poor Professor Pigou, who was still alive when I went up to King's College Cambridge in 1956, was roundly attacked for his views about wage adjustment, as were others who concerned themselves with micro-economic arguments and measures.

The Keynesian prescription offered an answer not just to capitalist collapse, but to unemployment in particular. Revolution might be not too particular about following Marxian chronology. It might not wait for ultimate capitalist crisis but could spring out of the fright, anger and hunger of mass unemployment, of millions of people without jobs, without any idea how to create their own occupations and without the means even if they had the ideas. Unemployment then truly meant severe deprivation as well as complete loss of dignity and status, except for the very lucky few who had something to fall back on. But most people didn't and it never seems to have occurred to policy-makers that there could be any change in this 'natural' condition of things for the vast majority of the population.

For the liberal who wanted the defeat of Marxism it was therefore not just desirable, but imperative that a strong and efficient government should swing into action with centrally inspired measures to boost purchasing power, multiply jobs and head off the dark and bloody Marxist threat for good. One can well understand how this life raft, once gained, was not a spot which the liberals or the Conservative party of the late thirties or the immediate post-war period, who had had a bad fright, were going to abandon lightly or in a hurry. Central economic strategy was needed, demand could be and had to be managed and maintained, to head off something much worse and more dangerous.

Why did the Keynesian route, which was obviously centralist, seem so attractive and the route via micro-solutions, via measures to make the labour market work, seem so impossible? Why did so many people come to reject the classic economic proposition that if both wages and prices adjusted downwards, then equilibrium could be regained at levels of high employment?

The answer has to be the one to which Keynes returned several times, that since wages meant living standards, or indeed subsistence standards, there was no way in which unions could or should accept general wage cutting. Even if they did, this would simply cut purchasing power and exacerbate the situation. He could see no means by which alternative purchasing power could be channelled through individual hands, for instance through wider capital distribution, and no likelihood of local and smaller scale enterprise growing in place of the depressed great industries all around the nation. The national economy, the nationally based unions, the national financial institutions and the centralised system of administration in Britain were simply not organised in a way that could allow anything of that kind to happen. Anyway, it clearly was not happening. Some new practical and effective answers were needed at central Government level and were available to be tried.

In the post-war world the Keynesian system seemed to work excellently. A whole science of central economic intervention blossomed. If the cost was a little mild inflation the benefit was much bigger, an amazingly high level of employment and steady expansion. If Keynesian macro-economic prescriptions could deliver these results then they must indeed be powerful and relevant, and well worth the degree of centralisation and state involvement which was required to run things smoothly.

However, by the 1970s, and even before the first oil price explosion of 1973, that world was coming to an end. The famous Phillips curves, the ultimate in scientific Keynesian management techniques, which instructed that there was always a neat trade-off between unemployment and the inflation rate, somehow seemed to stop working. Unemployment, as traditionally measured began to acquire a maddening direction of its own and to throw off obedience to central intervention, and that direction was upwards, quite regardless of the rate of expansion or the inflation in the economy. In fact the two phenomena of unemployment and inflation seemed to rise together, creating Arthur Okun's famous 'misery' or 'economic discomfort' index' (compiled by adding the unemployment and inflation rates together.)

However, at this stage there were still only a very few voices suggesting that perhaps the power of central and national governments to devise policies which would create economic wealth, provide jobs and secure stability was not quite as decisive as the macro-economists had claimed. Even fewer suggested that people might now be acquiring the power to do these things for themselves in a way they had been unable to, or were prevented from doing in earlier phases of industrial and technological development. Laissez-faire remained an extremely dirty word.

There were, of course, the monetarists who had some valuable insights to contribute but, as is often the way, claimed much too much for their proposals. Worse still, they seem to have been infected by the same illusions about the powers of central government to manipulate and control aggregates as their Keynesian predecessors. A balanced monetarist advocacy would have perhaps rested on the point that national economies were amorphous concepts at the best of times, that some central Government powers to manoeuvre the economic and financial aggregates were indeed very primitive and crude and that a sensible and limited ambition should be to try, roughly, to balance the annual budget maybe over a three or four year cycle with some prudent borrowing for public capital projects. However, the main forces which would provide stability to the economy, which would create work and generate growth would be found at the micro-level and should be fostered at that level. That would have been the sensible and restrained monetarist approach, and it was one which several people advocated for the United Kingdom, when the new 'monetarist' government took office in 1979 – although in vain initially. The level pullers it turned out, were still in charge even though the economic doctrines had changed and even though the aggregates requiring control had changed. (We shall have more of this story to tell in Part VI).

However, even if monetarism had been associated from the start with a much more radical anti-centralism and far greater scepticism about macro-economics than it was, there would still have been another pro-collectivist force of formidable strength with which to contend on top of lingering Keynesianism.

Towards the end of the fifties J. K. Galbraith had published his biting attack on private sector affluence which seemed to produce a whole new agenda for the supporters of enlightened state power.[1] Without intervention from the centre, Galbraith claimed, the prospect opened out of unending public squalor and lack of good public facilities, of inadequate research, of investment in the 'wrong' industries (the right ones being determined by senatorial wisdom from the centre) and other deviations.

Here was a menu to give those who wanted state power without state bullying, and who were getting a little uneasy about incipient 'stagflation', a whole new meal. Those who wanted less government or smaller government now had to contend with two formidable arguments, not one. A smaller role for the centre in managing the economy might not only risk the return of the Marxist nightmare of instability and deficient purchasing power. It would also allow the perpetuation of a commercialised, polluted society of unutterable squalor. The

1. J. K. Galbraith *The Affluent Society*.

environment would be destroyed, the quality of life fatally
undermined. Huge market-dominating firms – the 'technostruc-
ture' would control economic activity and squeeze out the
smaller and more fragmented parts of the economy where the
market could still be said to operate. For the entrepreneur and
the smaller enterprise there could be less and less room. It
would wither away.

What was the answer to this? The monetarist and market
economists at first appeared to have none. A firm commitment
to deregulation and a strong drive against monopoly might help
but it seemed inevitable that capital would be concentrated in
few hands and large firms, who would shape consumers' lives
and that Galbraith was right. If we wanted better public facilities, better education and health care, higher quality transport,
more efficient power utilities and cleaner streets, then clearly
the state would have to get more and not less involved in their
provision.

But there was an error in all this, the error of centralism, of
not perceiving the immense and combined pressure of markets,
social attitudes and technology in draining power and the
capacity to control away from the state and away from the
macro level. It was a mistake that the new sort of macro-economists were bound to make because they were still not aware
of the real nature of the change going on. They still believed
that powerful people at the apex of the modern industrial state
were needed to deliver public services as Galbraith himself
believed. And they still assumed that large institutions such as
the unions, the major pension and insurance funds and the
major national 'network' industries, like electricity generation
and gas and telephones, would have to continue in place,
whether under a monetarist or Keynesian regime. It was
certainly the all-pervasive assumption in Whitehall when I took
over at the Department of Energy in 1979, as we shall see in later
chapters and it certainly still colours much of the Government's
industrial thinking.

But as we shall also see, these assumptions turn out to be no
longer correct. Smaller and less centralised systems of social
provision are possible and indeed more efficient, if allowed to
grow. Private enterprise, often on quite a small scale now seems
able to provide public services in a more innovative and sensitive way than large bureaucratic institutions. Supposed economies of scale turn out not to be, and the economies of miniat-

urisation which are, if anything, even more spectacular, begin to dominate.

The industrial landscape which Charles Sabel found when he visited Northern Italy, mentioned in Chapter 4, is one which was not supposed to come into being according to the Galbraith diagnosis. Small, disorganised, almost anarchic firms, operating in full market conditions, were supposed to be disappearing under the heel of the great oligopolies of big business.

But ideas are now marching the other way. The whole attempt by Galbraith and his generation to depict national economies in terms of market and planned sectors, small business and giant dominating firms, is beginning to look oddly out of date.[1] So is the argument, which seemed so conclusive, that big and interventionist national government was vital to achieve the main economic and social goals, establish full employment, organise basic industry, infrastructure and services and generally manage the economy.

A social and industrial landscape is emerging through the mists of argument, and of old beliefs clashing with new and visible realities, which does not seem to have the Galbraithian features at all. The central powers he believed were essential to promote economic and social welfare are beginning to look both inefficient and unnecessary. Things can be done better on a smaller scale. The centre is falling apart. So both to the problems and worries of the Keynesian generation of macro-economists about unemployment and instability, and to the Galbraithian concern about 'inevitable' private monopoly power, we are now beginning to see the outlines of answers which are neither Keynesian nor monetarist. Nor do they rely on almost magically refined powers of control and management by central government. These answers fall into three groups, all of which we will be exploring in depth in later chapters.

1. To meet the Keynesian worry about demand deficiency and instability there comes the prospect of the share economy, of widespread capital ownership in support of wages and salaries, and of a vastly more flexible labour market which can adapt much more quickly to cyclical conditions (providing central governments do not maintain too many obstacles in the way). Wages *can* move up and down, and capital *can* compensate and ensure that purchasing power is well dispersed and

1. See J. K. Galbraith *The New Industrial State*.

the best conditions for local enterprise and new business growth created.

2. To the Galbraithian worry about public squalor comes the answer that the squalor can be overcome, but that central government and bureaucratic agencies are not the best instruments through which to do it. Markets are not being suffocated by big business – or need not be – and can deliver high quality 'public goods' with increasing sophistication.

3. Much of this is because of a third 'answer' which both Keynes and Galbraith can be fully forgiven for not even beginning to imagine – not least because even today many policy-makers have not grasped the full implications either. This 'answer' comes from the astonishing, revolutionising world of micro-electronics, which weaves new networks of information and power, which destroys the information monopoly of central governments, which creates vast new information flows, which makes markets infinitely less controllable and stratified, but infinitely more flexible, which creates an entirely new, more comfortable and more adaptable pattern of work for almost all and which, above all, changes the way to which economies behave. In the next section we now venture into this new landscape and discover its contours and features. To many people they are already familiar, even obvious. But to those who remain wedded to macro-economic management, to heavy central government intervention and to tight national economic control they will not be so obvious, and probably not welcome at all.

PART III

The Centre falls Apart

'Things fall apart; the centre cannot hold.'
W. B. Yeats, *The Second Coming*

CHAPTER 8

Electronic Erosion

In this part of the book we are going to try to show how the encroachment of new ideas, the hard and detailed impact of micro-processor technology on industry and commerce and the revision of social attitudes which is extensively bound up with this, are combining to bring about fundamental change in all aspects of economic life and therefore in the problems facing government.

We are heading out into unfamiliar terrain for those brought up in the belief that government has the answers to the major social challenge of the day. To say this may sound merely as if the struggle of ideas and philosophies is about to enter yet another round in the battle between collectivists and liberals, between central planners and supporters of market economics, with either side taking up the familiar positions.

But as we have seen it is not as simple as that. What we are now witnessing is not just another replay of the old conflict between one set of doctrines and another. There now seem to be forces at work undermining the position of the centralists which come from an entirely different quarter, which greatly reinforce the case for market economics and the price mechanism against the planners but which are so powerful that they take the whole situation far further than many of the market theorists, and especially the monetary engineers who ride with them, appear to have understood.

It is now the onset of micro-electronic technology, and the amazing revolution in the scope, flow and handling of information which it brings with it, which is gnawing away at old convictions about the proper role and duties of government. Large scale administration is ceasing to be either workable or necessary. The computer age, which many people feared would bring more power to central authorities, is turning out to be a force for dispersal, a natural ally of market economics and an agent of variety and, possibly, some anarchy. It is creating, in short, a highly revolutionary process which aids and abets, and even overrides, the forces which have already long been at work undermining the collectivist approach. In his 1985 Reith Lectures the OECD economist David Henderson described how his profession had long tended to regard questions of resource allocation and the way markets actually functioned as a second-tier issue. Their greater concern was with big national issues of government policy, which aggregates to control, how to expand demand, the size of the national budget deficit, the control of the money supply.[1]

His suggestion was that the time had come for a change of emphasis. It might now be that the key to many of the things which the macro-economists had been struggling for several decades with such limited success to achieve, such as full employment with price stability and steady economic growth, lay more with resource allocation and the freer use of markets than with either Keynesian or monetarists 'macro' techniques.[2]

What he did not go on to describe were the reasons lying outside economics why this might be so. Amongst economists, as he rightly observed, there were plenty of arguments leading one to doubt whether macro-economics could deliver what its proponents originally hoped and suggesting the need for a new approach. But that leaves an awkward and central question unanswered. Why should markets now work better than they did in the 1930s? Why in particular should labour markets function any better? There may well be more talk from national governments about de-regulation and controls on monopolies, unions may be quiescent. But these are surely slender grounds upon which to attempt the overthrow of the whole Keynesian prescription and of a large part of monetarist faith as well. There seems to be something missing from the Henderson thesis, welcome though its insights are.

The problem, I believe, is that like many economists Henderson gives insufficient weight to the real forces that are carrying his cause along. Outside the world of debate between economists changes are at work which are altering the entire context in which that debate is set. Unless there are understood, unless the explosive impact of micro-electronic technology, and other miniaturising and transforming technologies bound up with it,

1. David Henderson. Reith Lectures 1985. 'Innocence and Design'. Lecture No. V.
2. Ibid.

is appreciated, then the economists may again find that their diagnosis is wrong, that their advice is wrong and that the policies they urge on governments, and which governments then try to carry out, are disastrously deficient.

The process of technological change is now so pervasive, and is affecting so many different aspects of life and work, that it is intensely difficult to try and disentangle and examine some of the separate parts. Most of this book, including the later sections on personal and family attitudes, on changing views of work and the changing role of women in economic life, are connected with it.

However, let us take one thing at a time. In this part of the book we are going to concentrate on the industrial and commercial scene and on some of the more immediate ways in which electronic technology is carrying us into a new landscape. The first major new factor on the scene which needs to be assessed is one to which observers outside central government have given little attention and often ignore altogether. This is the extraordinary extent to which modern information technology is dispersing knowledge and data, rather than concentrating it, and in doing so, actually weakening rather than strengthening the power and authority of centralised administration and centrist attitudes.

The following chapter goes into this development and gives some examples of how it is already happening in Britain, although of course it is a process which central administrators are not too keen to acknowledge and to which Ministers find it intensely difficult to adapt. The whole Parliamentary system, and the doctrine of Ministerial accountability tend, after all, to push the other way and to press Ministers and Whitehall Departments into appearing to be responsible for everything going on in the economy. Explanations that Ministers are not accountable for, or in any way able to influence, say, big industrial events like a business collapse or a factory closure or do not know about work conditions in a particular area or industrial sector, or cannot control major developments in the market place, such as soaring fuel prices, for example, are always received extremely badly and often with total disbelief. The situation is made no easier by the almost inevitable tendency of hard-pressed politicians to take some of the credit for favourable developments, such as lower inflation or the rapid emergence of some highly successful new industry, or some major new

investment project, when it is clear that central government
could have had very little influence on the events in question
and may not even have known about them until its attention
was directed to the right spot.

The second feature on which we will focus is related in its
effects to this one. We need to be aware of the unmanageable
information over-load at the centre of government, combined
with a precipitous decline in the quality and reliability of that
information, as activities in the economy and society become
much more diffused, less susceptible to organisation and docu-
mentation and generally harder to track. It is not just most
economic forecasts that are wrong. It is official figures telling
the centre what is supposed to be happening currently, or even
what is supposed to have occurred in a past period, that are no
longer presenting a reliable picture. This is of course the
complete opposite of the nightmare prospects of an all-
powerful, all-knowing, all-intrusive state against which Orwell
and Huxley warned.

The third feature on which we will spend some time is the
powerful fragmentation process affecting the industrial structure of advanced societies which communications technology,
data handling techniques and the miniaturisation of processes
has made possible. This has begun to alter the entire balance
of the arguments on the issue of economies of scale, and on
the issue of central state ownership, it makes possible a more
flexible and less concentrated pattern of production and
exchange than anything that has existed since the early days of
the industrial revolution. (It is also one of the factors revolutionising the labour market and therefore personal lifestyles, as we
shall see in Part 4 of the book).

Finally, in this Part of the book, there will be a look at a
development which, from the point of view of policy-makers
inside national administrations, is potentially the most baffling
of all – the internationalisation of both information and finance
through micro-electronics. Again, one needs the reminder that
this is not futurology, it has already occurred. Computer technology and person-to-person electronic linkages have already
established information networks which by-pass the formal
heirarchies of state authority and have now effectively global-
ised the world's financial system. Capital, at first in large
amounts handled by corporate treasurers, but was increasingly
in small individual amounts, can be switched almost instan-

taneously from account to account and country to country, leaving national policy-makers with a harder and harder task in trying to retain local control of economic and financial developments – and a much harder task, too, in trying to convince sceptical electorates that they are in control and retain authority.

When we have completed our survey of these areas, which are really all parts of the same panoramic picture of economic life and social behaviour being transformed by technology, it will be time to assess some of the consequences both for government generally, specifically for the present Government and its policies, and also for ourselves, the members of this now utterly changed society in which we live and work.

CHAPTER 9

Scaling Down

No one would dispute that modern industry is changing its shape and structure. One can see that with one's own eyes in the new industrial parks as well as on the older industrial estates. Factories are becoming neater and smaller. Often they have no chimneys. Inside they are much quieter and cleaner, more like ordinary warehouses or office buildings. And almost every industrial area is now sprouting a crop of small industrial units as well. Hardly anyone is building vast factory complexes anymore and the existing very large units are scaling down. A process of physical miniaturisation seems to be going on throughout almost all parts of the industrial system.

And yet in one sense this appears to be flatly contradicted by what is reported in the media about happenings in industry. All the stories are of take-over battles between already gigantic conglomerates, of colossal financial amalgamations, of vast new investment projects. Everything associated with defence and the defence supply industries appears to involve very large sums and resources indeed. So does much of the discussion about the energy industries and energy supply, where the central government remains deeply entangled and where the language is all of national networks, integrated systems and long-term planning.

Much of the talk in European policy-making circles, too, continues to be in terms of large-scale policies. Until quite recently the whole intellectual climate in Brussels seemed to favour centralisation and ever-increasing industrial scale, often on the grounds that this was vital if Europe was to compete with America and Japan. Admittedly, the mood is now changing in thinking about European questions, but this has not yet been much reported.

This picture of industrial activity growing in scale has been reinforced by the way in which the Japanese scene has been presented in Europe. Travellers bring home tales of a Japan dominated by huge combines employing workers in jobs for life in disciplined hordes, the whole pattern being tightly coordinated at the centre by the Ministry of International Trade and Industry. The interesting but often ignored fact is that almost nine out of ten Japanese workers work in firms employing less than three hundred people.[1] Japan is in reality a nation of small and very small – 'micro – businesses. Its large and more visible parts rest on a huge cushion of sub-contractors, family firms and miniature undertakings.

In the 1970s some pioneering studies were made in Britain of another 'miracle' economy, Germany, where the prevailing wisdom had it that rationalisation and size were the driving power behind German economic success. Graham Bannock, conducting research for the Anglo-German Foundation, found that in the industries selected for research, German firms were far less concentrated than British and a far greater proportion of both output and employment was generated by a mass of extremely small enterprises.[2] He also showed that the alleged economies of scale used to justify a great deal of British industrial policy thinking did not exist in the German experience.

That was a decade ago. Since then the message has begun to reach parts both of British industry and the British policy-making machine in Whitehall. Since the publication of Bolton Report on small business in 1971[3] the figures suggest that the long decline in the numbers employed in small business has been reversed. Well over 90 percent of all firms employ less than 100 people. Moreover, the figures do not take full account of the fast growing number of firms which are in practice one person, or maybe a married couple, the people who are creating the demand all over the country for the small industrial units about which until recently neither planning authorities and local councils nor private developers showed much interest but which they have now suddenly discovered.

The impression that industry is nevertheless all about size and concentration is obviously fostered by the way it is publicly reported. Big happenings and battles involving billions, with powerful boardroom dramas, clashes between huge multi-

1. Institute for Labour statistics, Tokyo, 1985.
2. See *Smaller Business in Britain and West Germany*, published by Wilton House for the Anglo-German Federation, 1976.
3. Small Firms Committee of Enquiry, Cmnd 4811. Nov. 1971.

national enterprises and all the attendant excitements make irrestible copy. The British newspaper business is itself still very centralised in London, both physically and culturally, and likes to present things in sweeping national terms. Even as these words are being written there are signs that this Fleet Street domination is crumbling apart and that economic forces are about to give us a far less centralised and more fragmented newspaper industry, but these are early days and we may expect the 'big is beautiful' atmosphere to prevail in daily newspaper reporting about British industry for a while yet.

The Whitehall policy-makers also have another excuse for remaining pre-occupied with large-scale industrial issues, since these have been the problem areas left on government's plate. When the Conservatives were in opposition in Britain in the 1970s it was the hope of some of us that we could do away with a Ministry of Industry altogether. We saw that the Germans seemed to be able to get on quite well without an industry department in Bonn, so why did we need one?

In practice, when the Conservatives took office in 1979 this idea had to be shelved while the government struggled with the appalling problems of a highly centralised steel industry, a highly centralised coal industry, centralised car-making, electricity generation, gas distribution, telecommunications, and a host of other heavily concentrated industrial sectors. It is no surprise that with all these in the political headlines the impression is left that industry is all about bigness and that its affairs can only be tackled on a national scale. Nor is it surprising that the very welcome shift of direction emphasis that has in fact taken place in parts of government thinking towards the smaller end of business and towards acceptance that this may actually be the more significant part of the economy, is still largely overshadowed. The Galbraith analysis, with its overwhelming emphasis on large corporations and 'the planning sector' still tends to be the conventional wisdom.

Yet we have solid reasons for knowing that all is not as it seems and that what we hear and read in such traditional terms about industry is increasingly superficial. Peter Drucker has pointed out that while for most of recorded economic history primary commodity prices, including energy prices, have slumped when industrial economies flag and have soared when they boom, throughout the first half of the eighties this rule

has been reversed.[1] Something fundamental seems to have
changed in the appetites and behaviour of industry. With
growth all round and near boom conditions in Japan and the
United States primary product prices – whether coffee, cocoa,
tin, copper, oil or other minerals and metals – have remained
flat or have fallen over the decade. His conclusion, which seems
inescapable, is that the raw materials needs of growing industry
have radically altered. 'We may be witnessing' he suggests 'a
historical change and the first major impact of the shift from an
energy economy to an information economy'.[2]

A recent economic white paper from the Japanese Ministry
of International Trade and Industry puts things less hesitantly.
The growth of the service sector, it asserts, is promoting a new
degree of stability in the Japanese economy and reducing the
tendency to fluctuation. 'With no limitations in the availability
of resources and energy on the horizon' it continues, 'external
factors are likely to be more stable than they have been in the
past decade'. Noting that the investment cycle is also moving
in 'smaller waves' than before, the White Paper concludes that
Japan is entering 'a new age of growth', with less cyclical vola-
tility and with radical changes in both the economic structure
and patterns of work.[3]

Of course, as Drucker also points out, there are still plenty
of industries and technologies which are energy-hungry and
gulp up raw materials faster than they increase output. But
these tend to be the older or stagnating ones, which often fall
back on central government for help and social support. The
growth areas are information-intensive rather than energy or
raw materials-intensive. The technologies are getting smaller –
miniaturising – and so are the industrial structures in which
they are applied. This applies not just to the 'glamour' high
technology industries like data-processing (which used to need
big bureaucracies), electronics, high-temperature ceramics, low-
energy chemical processes, robotics and bio-technology related
industries. It applies to every product process which makes use,
somewhere along the line, of the miraculously miniaturising
effects of the micro-chip. Whether the product is a screwdriver,
a piece of furniture or a sky-scraper, the machines which make

1. *Wall Street Journal*, 9.1.85.
2. Ibid.
3. '*Issues for a New Round of Growth*'. Economic White Paper from M.I.T.I., Tokyo
1985.

its components, or which make the machines that do that, are getting smaller and much more flexible. Small firms can thus compete far more effectively with large ones.

Once the old and supposedly incontrovertible arguments about economies of scale collapse, and it becomes both feasible and economically sensible to organise production and services in smaller units, then all sorts of pressures begin to operate within the existing 'big industry' structure which surface readings and orthodox methods of collecting industrial information do not pick up. We do not really have an accurate picture of the ways in which big firms are changing themselves from inside in response to these new economic and technological pressures. Perhaps we never will, since the processes will, by definition, be so disparate and varied. But there is little doubt that most large firms, unless they are fast asleep, are trying to contract their central staffs, disperse or decentralise their operations and make far more use of sub-contractors, outside consultants (who may have been employees earlier) and outside suppliers generally. This applies not just to components but to services such as pay systems, office maintenance, computing work, internal information services and other operations which in an earlier era would have been regarded as things which had to be done, without question, 'in-house'.

Robertson reports on the rise of what he calls 'intrapreneurship' in both Sweden and the United States[1] the process by which previously large firms hive off bits of themselves into separate entrepreneurial undertakings. This is not just a question of delegated budgetary responsibility and creating profit centres but of setting up distinct mini-companies to perform a quite central part of the parent firm's production process, or to undertake the firm's research activities or develop a new product line. There is no reason to suppose that large British concerns are not thinking the same way. However, if they are, they will regrettably be still finding that much of public policy remains fundamentally hostile to these trends. The essence of intrapreneurship, as of other so-called auto-dynamic business activities, is to permit and encourage self-employment, doing one's own work, often geared to one's own time schedule. Yet the British tax administration remains resolutely set against self-employment and regards tendencies for it to grow with great

1. *Future Work* page 157. Gower, Temple Smith 1985.

hostility. When the British Institute of Directors recently called for a change in the laws to permit any employee who wished to change his or her status and become self-employed, this was greeted with stony disapproval as a dangerous and eccentric proposal.[1]

It is often asserted that the energy industries are the one sector where fragmentation and miniaturisation can have no impact, where big units are unavoidable and where Governments are bound to continue with their very deep involvement. Certainly this was the unquestioned assumption which confronted me when I became Secretary of State for Energy in Britain in May 1979. Most of the immediate problems which faced me had to be handled in this context. In those days (we are speaking of half a decade ago) it was 'unthinkable' that the coal industry could ever be fragmented or taken out of central state ownership. The National Union of Mineworkers would never allow it, even if it was technically feasible to consider a return to separate coal companies. Indeed the then still vastly powerful, dominant and nationally organised coal union could and did veto any liberalisation of coal imports which might have threatened the position of a single British monopoly supplier.

The same sort of thinking was applied to electricity generation and to power station building. Power station designers had accepted the almost unchallenged view that power stations had to be gigantic. The nuclear stations that the Government was being asked to approve, as the 'owner' of the dominant power company, were being priced at around £2 billion each in today's money. I can recall no one inside or outside Whitehall ever suggesting to me that electricity investment could be considered in a less massive, and therefore less hair-raisingly inflexible way. Building enormous power stations seems to have been one of the most central and favoured concerns of twentieth century collectivist economics. It is something which central state governments allegedly *must* do.

Giantism was also the overwhelming fashion in the gas industry and in oil. A break-up of the integrated gas industry in Britain, either vertically between wholesale and retail functions or by regions, was, it was claimed 'impossible', and this still seems to be the winning view even today in Whitehall. The

1. 'Labour market changes and opportunities'. Institute of Directors, December 1985.

oil industry might be international and therefore subject to big competitive pressures but few people seemed to doubt that it was a world for big players and many argued for state players, too. Even inside the new Conservative Government my initial proposals for carving new and smaller oil companies out of the state-owned British National Oil Corporation and the oil interests of British Gas, were greeted with hostility, especially from the Treasury, which had no conception of the forces at work in industry and was anyway preoccupied with heavily centralist attempts to impose discipline on the elusive national money supply. Plans to legislate for the privatisation of BNOC were endlessly delayed, first at the collective policy-making level and then at the level of the Government's business managers. Early plans for another new oil enterprise to be spun out of the British Gas Corporation's North Sea oil interests were dismissed as being unrealistic.[1] It was much better, said the Treasury planners, to hack bits off both BNOC and BGC and sell them for cash, than to pursue a positive policy of encouraging smaller, non-state units of enterprise in this field. My plans for encouraging new and smaller firms in the North Sea had rather more success initially, although, since then, the pressures from Whitehall, and especially from the fiscal policy-makers, seem to have grown again to discourage small firms which, it is assumed, are quite unsuitable by virtue of their size, for an effective role in the British oil industry.

The interesting point about all this is that since the early eighties, as the intellectual climate has changed and understanding amongst policy-makers has begun to catch up, albeit a bit patchily, almost every one of these assumptions about the importance of size in the energy industries, which seemed so solid, has come under severe challenge.

The major strike challenge from the National Union of Miners, which was bound to occur at some stage, and in anticipation of which a massive long-term programme of preparation and defence was initiated in 1980, has come and gone, leaving the British coal industry now wide open for reform. With the NUM veto on competition removed, all kinds of proposals for smaller coal producing companies, resting on private finance, and being aired and receiving serious consideration. Some

---

1. Eventually these saw the light of day with the setting up and flotation of 'Enterprise Oil' in 1984, three years afterwards.

suggestions have been for worker buy-outs of groups of pits; others for the grouping of certain pits and 'customer' power stations into marketable companies, with major British firms who already invest heavily in coal elsewhere in the world participating. None of these ideas were on the table for discussion in 1979. Today they seem like the obvious next steps to bring British coal production up to the required levels of efficiency and adaptability.

As for power station holdings, which always seemed to be the kind of 'lumpy' very long term investment which 'only governments can do', here, too, the perspective has changed. What has occurred in this area in the United States is particularly very instructive. Since American power utilities are privately owned most of them have had to seek their finance from capital markets. As the cost of a single power station with a capacity of, say, 1500 megawatts has soared into the billions, as the gestation period has lengthened with endless inquiries, objections and legal obstacles, and as delays and difficulties have multiplied over nuclear power stations in particular, investors have in effect gone on strike against the size and riskiness of such long-term projects. Give us, they have said, something smaller and less risky to back with a quicker pay-back. Had there been an alternative escape route of state finance, the industry would no doubt have taken it and continued to build giant stations on the grounds that no technological alternative option existed. Pressures of this kind are in fact already building up within the British Government and the largest generating board, the CEGB, in relation to power station needs in the 1990s. The fall in the price of crude oil from the wholly unrealistic levels to which they were pushed by politics in 1979 and 1980, adds a new complexity to power station planning, putting a question-mark in particular, on our new nuclear power stations such as the giant Sizewell plant.[1]

But in the American case there has been no opportunity to put the clock back in this way. Instead the technicians and designers have been compelled to use advanced technology in order to create small but economic power units to supplement

---

1. The Sizewell proposal is for a Pressurised Water Reactor station which will be the first of its kind in the United Kingdom. British rules, regulations and engineering idiosyncrasy have also ensured that it is virtually another prototype. With oil prices likely to stay low and interest rates high, it's starting date looks like being indefinitely postponed.

gradually the existing base system. The philosophies of **miniat-**
urisation and flexibility, have, under the compulsion of
necessity, been called into an area where the assumption had
previously reigned unchallenged that large and centralised
systems were essential. Engineers are now discovering that
the applications of miniaturised technology are explosive and
endless. Huge nation- or state-wide grids for supporting a
reliable service to millions of consumers of electric **current, or**
telecommunications or gas supplies or even mass **transport**
facilities are becoming unnecessary and inefficient. **Although**
the firms which dominate both telecommunications **and gas**
distribution in Britain, British Telecom and the British **Gas**
Corporation, are passing into private hands as mildly **regulated**
monopolies, it is almost certain that the combined assault of
technology and market forces, each reinforcing the other, will
erode their monopoly positions quite quickly. Licensing **restric-**
tions and other devices designed to preserve the **monopoly and**
please the investor, are bound in due course, and **probably**
soon, to be undermined.

CHAPTER 10

Scaling Down: Further Aspects

The enormous dispersive forces operating on industry and economic life generally take on acute political significance in a society like the British when so many of the big industries and services have been both state-owned and heavily centralised and when the privatisation debate is now in full swing. Many arguments have been put up in favour of privatisation. The macro-economists have developed a specially close interest in this obvious source of funds and in the opportunity which sale of state assets provides to 'doctor' the figure of the Public Sector Borrowing Requirement (for example by financing extra public spending out of asset sales receipts).

But the strongest and most valid arguments for privatisation are the ones put forward when the word was first introduced to the British political vocabulary in my pamphlet *A New Style of Government* published by the Conservative Political Centre just before the General Election of 1970. There I acknowledged Peter Drucker's role in developing the privatisation concept and suggested that the policy was likely to develop in Britain, as the logical outcome of efforts to decentralise the functions of a hopelessly overloaded British central government. I argued that with the support of new technology, then just dawning, large areas of centralised industries and services could be safely put out to competition and private ownership, and that any required co-ordination could be achieved without the burden of central ownership and management of huge nationalised enterprises.

Having since then held Ministerial responsibility over four years for several of the largest nationalised industries I am many times more convinced of the imperative need to let these changes work through the whole nationalised sector. I do not believe that it is even now fully appreciated what a conservative and anti-innovative ethos a nationalised industry produces over the entire area of economic life which it covers. In effect, the British nationalised sector, composed of massive and inevitably centralised concerns, all with an in-built interest in preserving their huge structures, has sterilised a large part of the British economy. In railways, coal, gas, electricity and, until recently, telecommunications large single state buyers have been able to paralyse development and crush small business growth by dictating price and purchasing policies and by insisting on using 'in-house' suppliers to meet every need from engineering design and computing to office cleaning and catering.

The British Government's privatisation programme, which gradually gathered impetus after 1980 as these lessons also bore in on my colleagues, is therefore enormously welcome so long as it is recognised where the underlying rationale lies. Technology and market forces, operating in a wholly new context, are destroying the basic reason for these large industries to exist at all. As long as privatisation acknowledges this process, and does not try to resist it, the policy will be working with the grain of economic and social trends. Whether that has happened in the case of either British Telecom or the British Gas Corporation is a moot point. One can see the direct clash of policy interests. Sale of a virtual monopoly attracts the most receipts for the Exchequer and provides a good vehicle for the mass investor. It pleases the macro-economic strategists who believe they are influencing the economy with their central numbers and it undoubtedly helps spread the idea of personal capital ownership, which is a vital ingredient part of a post-socialist modern society, such as Britain could and should become. (We shall have more to say on this point in Part V).

But it is certainly not wise to stand in the way of fragmentation and decentralisation in these key industrial areas for the sake of better central funding and of trying to make figures which are inherently vague and imprecise add up precisely in the national budget. If the argument is that lower personal taxes can only be financed by asset sales, because the PSBR must be such-and-such and an overshoot would raise Britain's already high interest rtes, then this is almost certainly putting the priorities in the wrong order. As has been explained in earlier chapters, the forces operating on UK interest rates are largely international and uncontrollable by national government policy, while the PSBR is in practice an 'artistic' rather than a 'scientific' figure.[1] If the aim is to lower central government taxes in Britain, as it most certainly should be so as to allow a fully-occupied society to develop with minimum impediment, then this should be done anyway and not at the expense of equally vital policies for liberating key parts of the British economy or in order to shore up unbelievably precise central figuring in support of discredited macro-economic theories.

The same forces which are destroying the argument for having big state owned and run industries are also of course, destroying the argument, with which they have been bound up from the start, for having big, nationally organised unions. The most vivid example in Britain of this process at work is the weakening of the NUM and the growth of an alternative union, the Union of Democratic Mineworkers. But the trend is evident throughout the traditional parts of the British trade union movement and it has been skilfully reinforced by government measures which have removed the obstacles in its way (and the barriers against change to which union leaders of the old school have quite naturally desperately clung).

This is an area in which Conservative policy-making has been premeditated, careful and extremely well-attuned to the changing industrial structure and the new work patterns going with it. While, as we shall see in a later chapter, many things remain to be done in the way of policy measures to fit in with a society of fewer full-time, full-career employments, on the trade union legislative side steps have been very positive. Beginning with the so-called 'Stepping Stones' strategy devised by the Conservatives when in opposition in the seventies, the policy has been implemented under successive Secretaries of State at exactly the right tempo. What was considered almost indecent comment about baronial trade union power and control over nationalised industries a decade ago has now become commonplace observation. Unionisation continues to serve many vital functions at the individual plant level. But against the powerful pressure now at work towards fragmentation and competitive market operations the old national trade unions can no longer hold together or act effectively. They are visibly disintegrating. Scargillism, which has come to mean in

1. Theoretically, of course, it is simply the 'difference' between forecast – or out-turn – revenues and public expenditure – two very large figures. In practice, many of the underlying figures and definitions are hazy and unreliable.

effect the rabid resistance to these new realities by all means at the disposal of traditional national union organistion, has been broken. That is the true and historic significance of the defeat of the NUM led by Arthur Scargill in the year-long British coal strike of 1984–85.

*   *   *   *

We must turn to one more area of British economic life to get a full picture of the industrial and business changes which are invalidating central government controls and creating a new and more dispersed environment. We need to take a look at the sector of the economy which occupies much the largest amount of space in our society and is the decisive influence on our surroundings and our countryside – namely agriculture.

There has been an exodus from British farming. In 1950 there were approximately half a million farm holdings. In 1984 the figure was around 230,000.[1] The vast majority of those that have left have been smaller farmers, those with less than a hundred acres, most of them unable to make a living any more, as they once could, out of livestock.

Throughout the post-war period it has been the policy of successive British Governments to encourage farm amalgamations, and to do so by a whole range of grants, tax allowances and general support policies which promote bigness. In a sense it is as though the great eighteenth and nineteen century enclosure movement has never stopped. Tenant farms have been taken back into large estates, new tenancies curtailed. Sky high land prices have shut out new entrants. Farmers and farmworkers, as well as those manning all the trades which supported a smaller scale kind of agriculture, have vanished in enormous numbers from the land and from the industry.

It used to be argued that this trend towards size was desirable on grounds of efficiency. More food was needed and large farms showed the way to cut costs. Then, after 1973, when Britain joined the European Community, it was also pointed out that the Common Agricultural Policy, when applied to the British situation, had an even more powerful reinforcing effect in the same direction. Perversely, a system which on the Continental mainland was chiefly designed to preserve the small

1. *Annual Review of Agriculture.* 1986.

peasant farmer, did the opposite in Britain. It preserved the big boys and made life even harder for the smaller unit.

The reason for this was, and remains, that the CAP is intended to support the status quo in the farm structure. In France and Germany this has meant strengthening the position of hundreds of thousands of small farmers who have mastered the act of combining pocket handkerchief farm operations with other jobs and incomes and who find that with heavy price supports for their farm products things just tick along nicely. In Britain, the enclosure movement, and the impact of deliberate Government policies which continue to this day, has been to create a quite different status quo, one in which large farms dominate and account for over eighty per cent of farm output.

It is upon this already concentrated scene that the CAP has been brought to bear in Britain. Since the essence of the CAP system is to encourage more production and to relate rewards to output, the impact on Britain has been predictable. Enormous incentives have come into play to go for still larger output, to seek maximum economies of scale, to use every conceivable chemical and technological device to enlarge production. This has duly occurred. Agriculture has become very big business indeed. Its affairs are negotiated centrally and at a very high level between farm representatives and the government. Far from being a fragmented industry of sturdily independent people it has become in practice a very centralised and highly dependent sector. Only at the fringes, in the Western and Northern hill farming areas of the country, can one see the vestiges of a previous order, with small livestock farmers struggling desperately against soaring input costs to make ends meet. The contrasts with the patterns and lifestyles of the great farming estates in the eastern half of the country could hardly be more startling.

Now, in the last five years, the farming scene which brought such enormous prosperity to some has begun to fall apart. The claim that more food production is essential will no longer stand up. The world is now awash with colossal food surpluses, especially of temperate food products. New agricultural technology is vastly increasing yields without incurring the high costs of massive chemical applications that were previously necessary. American farm potential has soared. India is growing all its own grain and even exporting. The European agricultural policy, by pitching grain prices too high and then in effect taxing imports from elsewhere, has generated astronomical mountains of excess production. Even the Soviets, who could once be relied upon to mess up their harvests and need imports, have begun to get things right.

An additional argument used to justify continued high production in Britain has been that the nation must be self-sufficient. But that point, too, carries much less weight. In the 1940s it was a view point to be treated with respect. But now, almost half a century later, with an integrated and over-supplied world food market, and with weapons technology making that kind of war meaningless, it makes no sense at all.

As a result, the political pressures have built up on the farmers. A ceiling has already been imposed on open-ended receipts for open-ended dairy production and that has driven some of the more marginal farmers to the wall. It is a ceiling which could be lowered further. And it can only be a matter of time before the squeeze is put on cereals. The smallest farmers are probably able to survive the new pressures for a while by going back into sheep farming, where for the time being a living is to be had. The very big landowners were always bound to be better placed to absorb substantial cutbacks without discomfort.

The farmers who are really hit are those in between, the yeoman farmers probably with several hundred acres, inescapably high costs and falling receipts. If they are unlucky they will also have large loans fom the bank at high interest rates, taken out against the security of land of which the value is now shrinking, as big investors get out of land and high-profit agriculture becomes a thing of the past.

For many medium size farmers it seems as though the bottom has dropped out of their world. The security they could draw from the knowledge that their production was always 'wanted' and would therefore be strongly subsidised and protected has given way to doubts about all official policy, both European and national. For some there is always the option of selling out to the neighbour who wants to grow larger. But there, too, the prospect is looking far less enticing as Government enthusiasm for amalgamations wanes and as an increasingly well informed and sensitive countryside lobby opposes the techniques of large scale farming, demands tighter planning controls and less brutal ecological methods, and generally questions the logic of larger units if food is already in such staggering surplus.

Others with an innovative flair have begun to get out of conventional farm production and diversify into other products, like organically grown food, or special farm produce, or to use their buildings for other purposes such as pony stabling, or leisure facilities or small industrial units. But of course this takes farmers head on into conflict with planning strategies and the jealous guardians of the greenest of green belts.

What the farmers are now entitled to have, in a world where producing more food in no longer the main requirement, is some indication from the Government and the taxpayer of the minimum level of support which rural agriculture can expect to keep it in being at all. This means defining policies which encourage farmers to diversify and which encourage farming at lower cost and therefore on a smaller, instead of a larger scale. It means devising policies which encourage greater planning flexibility and allow farming and modern light industry to live closer together. Certainly this could not be more offensive environmentally than the ugly and disfiguring towers and buildings of modern big-scale agro-business and would probably be much less so, especially if it was controlled, whereas a good deal of farm development is not.

Above all it means halting the commitment to scale in farming and therefore halting the remorseless drain in numbers out of agriculture. Perhaps it is fanciful to suggest that the trend could actually be reversed. But it certainly could be halted. Technology and the changing intellectual climate are doing their work here too. Big farms are no longer economically necessary in Britain, both because high production is no longer imperative and because modern technology allows smaller units to achieve the same cost savings. Just as much as in manufacturing industry and service enterprises, forces are at work in agriculture which can and will fragment the industry and which policy ought to help along the way. From the new landscape could emerge, and is already emerging, a new kind of working life for those in agriculture and on the land. As has already occurred in, for example, Bavaria, the two-job farm life could begin to become the norm. We could soon see farm-owners and their families dividing the week between work in some factory or service industry, on-the-farm work itself and other work involving the farm's assets, such as converting and running holiday cottages or managing leisure facilities or offering landscape maintenance services to others in the rural community.

Paradoxically, this is a kind of life and a kind of economic activity which could make farmers freer and more truly independent again than they have been for decades past.

CHAPTER 11

Miniaturisation: The Political Impact

Having surveyed some of the immense changes which have affected industry and society in the years since 1979, and since the time when the assessments governing much of current public policy were formed, we can now draw together the threads of this part of the argument and see where they take us.

First, it seems clear that the electronic technology which has so transfigured the industrial landscape already should be seen, and judged, as a liberating, deregulating force. Miniaturised computer power is freeing people from bureaucratic centralism. It is freeing people from centralised policies based on generalised national views about industry and the economy. It is freeing and loosening up the industrial structure generally and creating a large and unfamiliar new range of business opportunities. And it is freeing increasing numbers of people from rigid work patterns dictated by somebody else and fixed for life (or for a period of life delineated and laid down by society, regardless of personal inclinations and circumstances).

Some have argued that computers and the information revolution would have the opposite effect, that vast volumes of data would give bureaucratic authority more control over people's lives, concentrate industrial power and activity in huge global combines. They have suggested that, even in the home, the computer and the terminal would become the new tyrants, binding people indoors, cutting off social contact and creating societies of wired-up zombies waiting to react to electronically transmitted instructions from the centre.

If this was a correct assessment then one would certainly want to see government policy work to resist electronic applications and hedge computer usage around with all sorts of restrictions. But this is not the way things are turning out. Computer power is developing as a refreshingly disorderly force, weakening the centre and freeing both people and ideas.

Personal computers have spread far more rapidly than forecast precisely because they are seen as a way of releasing men and women from the routines of the past, both at places of work outside the home and inside the home; and freedom from rigid work routines of course means much greater freedom to develop other interests, to spend more time shaping personal and family life and less time being pushed around.

For the libertarian there really should be no doubt about which side to be on. The whole freeing up process should be strongly welcomed. One can understand the unease of the liberally-minded thinkers of the 1930s about the obvious inefficiency of markets and their tendency to jam up and reinforce enormous concentrations of wealth and power instead of promoting competition. It was no good, Keynes insisted, expecting markets to adjust either in the long run, in which we were all dead, or even in the shorter term.

The lesson of today is that micro-electronic technology makes markets infinitely more efficient. This is not just a matter affecting larger concerns. The computer now gives the smallest enterprise virtually the same capacities as the very large to manage its business, control its finances with total efficiency and to gain access to information and electronic services – via so-called 'value-added networks'. The policies for freeing markets and unwinding state control and influence which were until a very short time ago regarded as unthinkable now begin to look like much the most socially responsible course. Laissez-faire thinking, which was seen as futile or ineffective against the ravening beast of capitalism, dividing and destabilising society, could actually now have become the principle way of achieving the great goals of economic stability, a fully-occupied society, expanding prosperity and really effective and generous care and support for the weakest – goals which the collectivists in one guise or another have been struggling and promising for half a century to deliver.

The second point which needs to be made at this stage is one that has been made before but bears repetition. It is that we are dealing not with visions of the future but with the state of society today, here and now. Policies which do not recognise the new condition are not just in need of revision 'in due course' but are already inappropriate and often directly hostile to the freer pattern which is struggling to emerge. Examples are large-scale economic policies which treat the major economic aggregates – the 'demand' – as though they were precise and relevant entities rather than abstract ideas of increasingly dubious validity; or industrial policies which condone or actually encourage concentration and scale, or social policies which assume that people work in large organisations away from home with dependent employee status, or planning and environmental policies that treat business as though it was still a matter of large factories with smokey chimneys, or housing policies which discourage mobility and tie people to one place of work, education policies which teach people to expect others to employ them, policies which damage local enterprise and independence and try to reinforce central government control. The list is endless and we shall be returning to these questions in some detail in later chapters.

The difficulty in such a traditionally centralised country as Britain is that changes on the ground take an inordinately long time to come to the eyes and ears of the policy-makers in London. In the meantime a sort of 'pretend' politics takes over at the centre, with an uneasy awareness growing that things are no longer what they seem but with the governing process being carried on as though nothing had changed.

There was an example of this in the 1970s when consensus politics and deals with the trade unions in Britain were all the rage. Long after it had started to become clear that the leaders of Britain's major national trade unions no longer controlled their troops, and long after it was evident that most people were actually outside the so-called organised sector of employment anyway, Labour government policy continued to be pursued on the assumption that the unions spoke for all workers and that binding undertakings could be exchanged with them. Although the Thatcher wing of the Conservative party had little hesitation about pointing out the hollow absurdity of this kind of policy-making, it retained its strong adherents well into the eighties, even amongst Conservatives. There are powerful voices inside the opposition parties and outside party politics who still talk in this language today.

In the same way, a new kind of 'pretend' politics has grown up in support of policies and conditions which seemed sensible in 1979 but which have now been completely outmoded and by-passed by events. Things are simply not as they were. There is no broad alliance of support for, or confidence in, macro-economic 'solutions' to the major economic and social problems, no belief in, or wish to return to, the kind of full-time employment which politicians continue to promise lies round the corner, no wish or need to go back to the futile kind of central government intervention in order to control 'incomes' with which both academics and policy-makers still toy longingly, no neatly defined 'block' of corporate manufacturing industry which must somehow be boosted by centrally conceived policy, as so many industrial 'strategists' still argue so vehemently. A persistent and unshaken belief at the level of central and national administration that things have not changed in turn justifies policy attitudes towards industry and business which actively resist change and government procedures which greatly reinforce these attitudes. The quite excessive degree of official coordination which goes on between Whitehall departments, with everything down to an absurd level of detail having to be cleared by the Cabinet Office and the Treasury[1], is all designed for a world in which central government had a very different role, and was seen by the public in a different role, from the one to which it should now be adjusting. The more that the Treasury policy-makers wrestle with the unruly economic and financial aggregates, and the more that their political masters publicly commit themselves to control of these abstract and amorphous entities, the more idiotically detailed the central control of other departments becomes. And the more that central authority is weakened by the disorder, variety and diffusion of market forces in an electronic age, the more furiously the official machine tries to co-ordinate and unify central government activity.

The extraordinary contortions experienced by the major nationalised industries also illustrate this process well. In the previous chapter it was suggested that there was case enough on grounds of efficiency and scale for the nationalised empires to be dispersed and made subject as far as possible to competitive forces. But even if this case did not stand, the impossible contradictions between financial centralism practiced by the Government and attempts by state industries to be more flexible

1. It could also be argued that the growth of *ad-hoc* Ministerial committee, and informal Ministerial gatherings called at short notice, which has characterised much of recent government, reflects the same increasingly frenzied attempt by the Cabinet to respond to the high pressure stream of events for which Parliament and the press will call Ministers to account but over which they have ever-diminishing control.

would provide an unanswerable argument for privatisation on their own.

Before the 1979 General Election there was talk in Conservative circles of setting the nationalised industries clear financial targets and then leaving their chairmen and boards to get on with their tasks. But in Government after '79 all this was swept aside as corporate plans, investment plans, pricing policies, pay policies and the minutiae of senior management and board salaries were all crawled over in the utmost detail. Moreover they were examined and re-examined at several different levels. First the boards made their stab at these issues. Then the sponsoring department had a go. Then either the Treasury or a group of Ministers had their turn. Now, if the boards themselves of these enormous state companies, some of the biggest undertakings in Europe, are not wholly in command of every detail then this applies even more to the officials in Whitehall departments who are not even hired or trained to manage large businesses. It applies even more again to officials from the Treasury and other departments who may have no regular contact with the concern in question and of course it applies totally at the Ministerial level, where political awareness may be high but specialised industrial knowledge is minimal.

In effect, nationalised industries have found that they operate under three tiers of top management, on their own boards, inside their sponsoring departments and at the level of central departments and Ministers collectively. No large industrial organisation can possibly work this way and fewer and fewer top quality managers have been prepared to try and make any of them do so.

Thus while technology has been undermining the raison d'être of the great state industries and services, and in practice making them harder and harder to manage anyway, the lingering demands of the macro-economists have been coming at them from another angle, overturning their business judgments, arbitrally cutting their borrowing needs and whittling down their investment plans. It is small wonder that soon after 1979 some of the hapless chairmen of the nationalised industries were looking back nostalgically at their days under a Labour Government when they had been openly used as instruments of central social policy and they at least felt they knew where they stood.

Privatisation takes these large and important areas of the

economy outside the reach of the 'pretend' politics of the mid-eighties – a prospect that some of the leaders of these industries have come to welcome and eagerly work for. They simply cease to be subordinate instruments of central government's continuing longing to apply macro-economic solutions, to re-create a traditional form of full employment, to control incomes and to try and shape industry and services. This must be wholly advantageous for society's main economic and social goals, even if the hankerings at the centre remain.

Something of the same spirit of revision of view seems to have infected the European industrial strategy makers, who at one time favoured both big-scale European industrial inte-gration as 'the answer' to economic lassitude and massive inter-vention from the supranational centre which they dreamt the Community would become. Christopher Tugendhat, for eight years a member of the Brussels Commission (four of them as Vice-President) has described the way in which large-scale Euro-pean policies began to seem intellectually outmoded. The Euro-planners blue-prints, he writes, 'were drawn up when there was great faith in the merits and advantages of sheer scale, in industry and other walks of life, as well as in politics. . . . The future seemed to lie with the big battalions. As opinion in the member states turned against those ideas, so their European version lost credibility as well'.[1]

It has always seemed to me that the European idea, which I strongly support, makes most sense when it seeks to encourage the interests of regions and localities within the European area, of great cities and of industries and trade that want to expand business together. Whatever the nature of the great ideals which gave birth to the European Community, the process of inte-gration has in fact invariably beeen driven forward by forces which have by-passed large central national governments and which would probably have been stopped in their tracks if they had not done so. The main forces have been, first, the determination of very great national leaders that Europeans should work together, often in the teeth of the opposition of their respect in national political supporters, and, second, the market pressures originating with particular businessmen and firms which have driven their own way across national fron-tiers, again with precious little help from national adminis-

1. Christopher Tugendhat *Making Sense of Europe*, p. 84. Viking 1986.

trations. It is therefore very encouraging to see the preoccupation of leading Europeans switch away from fruitless attempts to push national governments into an even more centralist mould and towards efforts to make the European market work. It will be very difficult, and not much will be accomplished at official level, where it is still national governments, through the Council of Ministers, that really decide everything.

But below the official and governmental surface technology and market forces are working in their new and highly effective combination to invalidate national barriers and establish ever stronger and more complex trade relationships. It is a process with which national bureaucracies cannot mercifully keep up. The prime example of this is in the field of financial services and movements of capital funds round the banking system. Official attempts to liberalise financial services across frontiers have really got nowhere. Unofficially, and aided by electronics, European financial services are rapidly integrating and will shortly transform the European economic scene, creating new conditions for the spread of grass roots capitalism and local enterprise, in a way which national governments could never hope to do, even if they really wanted to.

But perhaps the best illustration of all of the tensions and conflicts that are now arising as the strong trends of the real world clash with the 'pretend politics' of steadily weakening central administrations lies in another area – the field of local government.

Since the early eighties the Conservative Government in Britain has been engaged in a messy and acrimonious struggle with local government which has left many people outside politics very puzzled. The battle has its origins precisely in the macro-economic centralism which has been described in earlier chapters, although it has been complicated by the excesses and incompetence of certain local authorities, by deep confusion about the proper role of local government in Britain, and by an unfair system of local taxation – the rates.

From the start the Treasury wish was to control the total amount which local authorities spent, both capital and current, as part of their attempt to try and control the national economic and financial aggregates. In fact the Labour Government of the seventies had also been persuaded that this was a legitimate and sensible thing to try and do. At first under the Conservatives a complicated harness was devised, based on a series of Whitehall

views about the proper amounts by which the annual expenditure of each authority should increase. Discipline on a local
authority which exceeded its centrally decided target was
supposed to be exerted by withholding chunks of the rate
support grant to which all authorities were in varying degrees
entitled, depending upon their estimated needs (again based
on a complex central formula).

The arrangement was indeed a lunatic one and Lewis Carroll
would have felt quite at home at some of the Ministerial gatherings when these matters were discussed. The Treasury would
lay down a total of the amount which they hoped local government would spend in a year and departmental Ministers would
then argue strongly for their slices of this total figure (i.e. how
much local authorities should spend on education, how much
on policing, on transport and so on). However, the arguments
were not about real budgetary figures at all. They were about
the figures which the macro-economic experts in the Treasury
needed to fit into their absurdly precise planning totals. The
only connection with reality, and with what would actually be
spent, was that deviations from the notional numbers argued
about at the centre would trigger the grant penalty system.

The mechanism, unsurprisingly, did not work at all well.
Somehow the high spending councils went on spending. The
Treasury centralisers therefore took their next step and now
proposed that local authority expenditure should be directly
controlled. This would be done by taking unprecedented
powers to control the level of rates set by a local authority, and
to cap them if they were too high for central government taste.
However this still meant that local government might escape
the stockade by using receipts from the sale of capital assets,
notably council houses (encouraged vigorously under another
very popular government policy) to finance expenditure.
Additional controls were therefore devised to limit the rate at
which local authority capital receipts could be spent. The grip
of the 'macro' men on local government activity was now
complete. Although the actual passing of the legislation in
Parliament was bound to create bitter rows I do not think much
of this would have mattered if the 'enemy' against which the
whole armoury of policies was aimed had merely been the
wilder and freer spending authorities.

The difficulty is that the assault on a wholly inadequate
system of local government and its finances has coincided with

an enormous upsurge of concern to see a better and more independent pattern of local government in society. More precisely, the weakening influence and effectiveness of big national bureaucracies is being matched by a growing realisation that enterprises can be successfully organised on a much more local and intimate scale. It has dawned that the preoccupations of the macro-economists, for example with employment, can now be met by the strong development of much more flexible local work patterns and that local communities can generally do much more than was previously accepted to achieve economic vitality and independence, rather than being vulnerable appendages of the national economic system. This change of perspective about local potential and local markets, which information technology and the shift away from large-scale industry has greatly reinforced, in turn creates the need for efficient and genuinely local administration in order to provide the right framework, back-up of public facilities and general support for internally driven regeneration. But those who now look to local government to fill this sort of role in our society find nothing of this sort. Instead they are confronted by a pattern of local agencies of government, some of them out of financial control, geared very much to demanding 'more' from the centre, interested in attracting branch industries from outside (which thereby increase local dependency) and largely uninterested in establishing the local conditions in which local markets, and local enterprise can really take off.

The British local government structure is riddled with this dependency mentality. It spreads to the political parties and to many of the outside experts who think they have the 'answers' to inner city decay and believe that those answers can be imported. But beyond the experts lie real people who are clearly beginning to think differently. As we shall see in a later chapter this different approach is revolutionising attitudes to ownership and control of productive enterprise. It is also shaping a new and far more positive economic role for local administration.

The challenge for the British Government is therefore to come up with reforms which will respond to this very strong demand, to create more independent and local government than anything that existed before. It may well be true that local government in Britain hitherto has in fact been no more than series of local agencies of the central unitary state and should therefore obey the central view. But that kind of view cuts less

and less ice with people who see the potential of locally
organised enterprise and want the official structure to support
their efforts.

The clear need is for a system which is independent of central
government grant support, except for very specific social and
transitional needs, with the power to raise revenue locally by a
reasonably fair method, and a range of functions which can be
financed by that revenue or by prudent borrowings. At the
same time, the freedoms and incentives need to be built into
the new local government structure which will make it a force
working all the time *for* rather than against local business enterprise. Since modern industry and services can all perfectly well
exist in residential areas and the separation of industry from
homes is now an outdated planning concept, and since, as has
been mentioned in Chapter 10, farming and agriculture are
becoming merged into the pattern of local enterprise and industrial development, future local government should certainly be
much freer to make its own planning rules than today's mood
of centralism in Whitehall dreams of allowing.

All this suggests that for a start the cost of the largest local
'function' by far – education – ought to be born outside the
local government budget.[1] Whether it should be born by central
taxation or by a quite separate and possibly mixed system of
local support, parental contributions and central taxation is a
matter which is already beginning to be debated between
traditional centralisers and those who see new opportunities to
localise genuinely our appalling educational system.

But the change would then leave local government functions
quite closely matched with revenue raising capacity. A cap or
ceiling on the level of rates which could be imposed on any
business over and above the equivalent of the domestic rate
might then be desirable as a business safeguard, at least during
the transition period. The outcome would be to create local
governments which could govern and stimulate local communities rather than crush them under a blanket of regulations and
restrictions, both local and national. It would also then attract
much higher quality participants.

This trend towards stronger localism is one to which the
Conservative Government must vigorously respond. In a sense

---

1. The 1986 Rate Support Grant to local government, at just over £11 billion,
   is about the same size as the total school budget.

it is no more than recognising what was always the instinct of non-collectivists in Britain, namely that independent and healthy local government could, and would if allowed, work to achieve the nation's social and economic aims better than elaborate central bureaucracy. The trauma of recent years has been the discovery that the existing system of local administration was neither healthy nor independent and totally failed to fill this aspiration. The trauma of today is that the potential of truly effective local government is suddenly much more visible to the public, even if not yet to the Whitehall policymakers, and the demand for such a system therefore much more insistent.

Local pride and interest, and the desire to have a system of government which works on a local scale in support of it, are all part of the procession of new pressures and problems which have begun to move across the landscape since the beginning of the present decade and which place quite new and very urgent tasks on the central policy-makers. It is a landscape in which giant-scale industries look out of place, in which great state enterprises lose their purpose and in which the habits and outlook of those who believe in strong state power feel increasingly uncomfortable. For them the ultimate paradox has now to be faced – that the major social problems of the age may actually be ones which central state power can no longer tackle and which a more dispersed, much less centralised system of industry, work and finance can meet more effectively.

This goes against the grain of political thinking across a whole range of issues where for five decades or more people of a serious bent of mind, concerned about the problems of society, have been taught to believe quite differently. Nowhere has this been more so than in the area which is, for most people, the most significant, the daily pattern of work and the attitudes and customs which shape and surrounds people's working lives. Here, too, we shall see that the old world has turned turtle and, with it, very many of the assumptions upon which policy debate and the construction of government policy continues to be squarely based.

PART IV

A Fully Occupied Society

'I was unemployed and did no work, paid or unpaid.'
Declaration on Form UB25 which a claimant for benefit must sign

CHAPTER 12

Work, pay and living standards in the new landscape

Neither employment nor unemployment are well documented in Britain. Many people believe that far more are unemployed than the official figures suggest. Many others believe equally strongly that the figures are grossly exaggerated. Facts are very sketchy about part-time workers and the self-employed (not surprisingly), and even more cloudy about employment and work in the informal sector of the economy (we will define and examine these terms later) and in the black economy, both of which lie at the edge of, or outside, the purview of official records and knowledge.

We can, however, start with one reasonably secure demographic figure – the size of the population of working age, currently given as 32 million souls.[1] There is a difficulty about even this apparently safe figure because it assumes that 'work' stops at the official retirement ages of sixty-five for men and sixty for women. However, as more and more men and women go on working, and want to go on doing something, long after these artificial cut-off dates, this makes increasing nonsense of the old concept of a national retirement age and of the special provisions and policies traditionally associated with it. But let us begin with those 32 million. Just under half of these are recorded as being in full-time jobs in somebody else's employment. These are the traditional 'employed people' economists and policy-makers talk about.[2]

About 6 million work part-time for somebody else. So they have employment, but of a quite different kind to the familiar sort – a fact which worries traditionalists greatly because they do not believe these are 'proper jobs'. Another 3.3 million are

1. 1986 Economic Trends.
2. Ibid.

shown as having no job, that is, no paid work, although Department of Employment figures show, oddly, that about 900,000 of these do not actually want a job.[1] This may be because they are already at work but wish to go on drawing social security support, a state which makes them law-breakers under the present systems of social support. Or it may be because they have given up the effort. We do not know. The official figures also show that another million or so would like paid work of some sort but have not got around to signing on the register – which is why those who want to make the most of the largely meaningless 'global' unemployment figure talk about 4 million unemployed in Britain.

Next, there are reported to be about 2½ million people working on their own account, the great army of self-employed. Again figures are hazy here and many of these may be people who are also working part-time for someone else, or are recorded as fully employed.[2]

What about the remaining 3–4 million? Are they all 'doing nothing'. Certainly not. That would be an absurd conclusion. Most of them are hard at what every normal person would call work, although the official statistics do not; looking after families, old people, disabled or ill people. Some may be working with intense energy in voluntary and unpaid jobs, using their own capital resources or some other income source to support their living standards. Those who literally do *no* work, and spend every day from waking to sleeping in the unalloyed pursuit of pleasure and leisure are the eccentric and rare few and probably number a few thousands. In fact in modern conditions it is hard to imagine anyone actually doing no work at all, paid or unpaid, compelled or voluntary, formal or informal, except the totally incapacitated.

When all this is added up a picture straight away emerges which is sharply at variance with convention. Half the workforce do not have 'typical' paid jobs. Half the workforce are not 'employed' in the sense in which the word is used and thought about in most discussions about jobs and employment. Moreover this assumes that the other half, who are recorded as being in full-time work, are just that. It seems most unlikely. Almost all of them will be 'working' in some way in the home for no

1. Ibid.
2. Ibid.

pay, as well as working for their employer. It is the rarity who will flop down after paid work each day and do nothing, or merely do something which is unquestionably a leisure activity. In other words, considerably more than half the 'work' actually done each day in our society is performed outside the formal sector, outside the 'employed' regime, and outside the sort of world towards which almost all employment policy has until very recently been entirely directed. We are thus worlds away from the simple and solid approach which Lord Beveridge, for example, was able to employ so confidently in his book *Full Employment in a Free Society*.[1] There, he used statistics of male full-time employment and unemployment in a number of specific industries as his raw material. He felt no need to question what lay behind them because he knew that a lack of full-time job for the male head of the household meant appalling deprivation in the conditions of the 'thirties – and in this he was broadly, if not wholly, correct. He was also completely confident that the State authorities were equipped and competent to tackle the huge tasks assigned to them in recreating this kind of all-embracing employment for nearly all males of working age.

Today things are very different indeed. Concern is great, but confusion is complete. This is because there is very little agreement as to what we should be looking at and about what we should be worrying on the unemployment front. The words 'employment' and 'unemployment' conceal very hazy concepts indeed. They wrap together two vital aspects of life, which it would be more accurate, and perhaps more illuminating, to consider separately – namely work and remuneration. The traditional way of thinking equates the two entirely. Without work, you starve. Work is income and income determines the standard of life. Jobs for all mean a decent standard of living for all. That is the thesis.

But even when we separate out the two elements, work done and income as a means of support (and for very many people these are indeed partially or wholly separate), there is very great ambiguity about what the words 'work' and 'income' actually mean and how they should be defined. For example, no one could question that one of the hardest and most wearying forms of work is bringing up a family and running a

---

1. George Allen and Unwin, November 1944.

home, as we have already implied by calling this activity work, which it is. Yet this kind of 'work' appears nowhere in the national incomes statistics. If people decide to spend less time in paid jobs and more time 'working' at bringing up their children, that shows up in the figures as less work done and more time spent on leisure.

The habitual way of looking at work is so deeply engrained that even its chief 'victims' seem unaware of its capricious absurdity. Quite a few young and newly married women, when asked what work they do, reply defensively that they do not work because they are kept at home looking after small children. What they mean of course, although the customary language has made it almost impossible to find the words, is not that they are idle but that nobody is paying them for their very arduous labours, or that nobody is paying them direct, at any rate. Income is coming from elsewhere – from the other partner in the marriage, from state credits and benefits, possibly from personal savings, maybe if the couple are lucky from the odd parental handout. But to these women and to most orthodox economic thinking, what they are doing is not really 'work'.

There is nothing very new or revolutionary about this odd view. 'Women's work' has always been extremely hard and rarely rewarded in cash or kind. James Robertson cites the example of the OECD survey of developing countries which found that in most of them the immensely arduous task of water-carrying, almost always the responsibility of women, simply did not figure. In Kenya, the survey found that 'since women have virtually no employment opportunities in certain pastoral areas of the country, the collection of water in these regions is excluded from economic calculations by government statisticians'. Had the work been done by men, the survey observes, it would be counted as work.[1] But of course the same double standard applies to many other kinds of 'work' as well. Washing, cleaning, mending the car, mowing the lawn, making the beds, shopping, clearing the gutters, carpentry in the garage to make new kitchen work tops, are all unquestionably work.

Professor Charles Handy of the London Business School has written a pioneering volume, *The Future of Work*[2] analysing and categorising these 'work' activities, according to whether they

1. Kathleen Newland in *The Sisterhood of Man*, (Norton), quoted by James Robertson.
2. Charles Handy, *The Future of Work* (Blackwell) page 41 ff.

are unpaid (and uncounted) or paid but carried out mostly at home, or paid and unrecorded (the black economy and the moonlighting side of life) or involving a formal place of work, a formal wage or salary and the formal label of gainful employment.

Professor Handy labels the first three of these informal categories the 'mauve' economy (paid, legal but mostly home-based), the 'grey' economy (domestic work, mostly unpaid) and the black economy. Together he argues that they constitute the informal sector of the economy, as opposed to the formal sector in which people 'work' for full-time wage or salary. In the formal sector people are 'employed' in the straightforward unambiguous way which Beveridge would have understood and which many policy makers, politicians and commentators still believe to be the only right and proper circumstances.[1] As we have seen, economists have traditionally been concerned only with this 'formal' part of economic life and activity. They have depicted it as the only part that matters and deserves the full application of thought in economic questions.

Handy also lists some of the enormous range of occupations which belong in the informal category – tasks which are performed mostly at or from home in the worker's own time, sometimes on a part-time basis, sometimes on a very full-time basis indeed – in fact much more full-time, going late into the night or starting long before breakfast, than the normal so-called 'full-time' factory or office job. Obvious examples are accountancy, specialist teaching, computer programming, many forms of journalism and authorship, research work, design work, telephone sales operations, all varieties of home and garden services, catering, craftwork, consultancy of all kinds, pottery, picture-framing, translating, proof-reading, dress-making, many kinds of financial services – the list is vast and always growing.

The pattern is changing very fast. People are on average spending more of their waking hours than a decade ago on 'home' work – misleadingly shown in the statistics as leisure; more people are doing work at home; more people are moon-lighting; more people are doing work both in the informal and the formal part of the economy at once, sometimes mixing 'black' undeclared work with officially recognised 'full-time'

1. Ibid.

employment, sometimes openly doing two jobs, sometimes deliberately doing part-time paid work, so as to have more time 'working' at family and household tasks, or at hobbies, or in voluntary work, which may well be equally vital even if not valued in the market place at a high pay rate. All this suggests that people are becoming much more adept at straddling the formal and informal sectors of the economy and in organising their lives so as to do more than one form of work or 'job'. Most married women with young children probably now fall into this category.

One of the remarkable things about the whole changing scene is that we do not need to look into the crystal ball to see it. This is not predictive guesswork which 'serious' analysts and 'realistic' policy-makers can brush aside whilst they continue to agonise about declining male manufacturing employment – which on conventional measurements has now been going on in Britain for twenty years – or to ask where the jobs will come from, or when will we get back to good old-fashioned full employment as they knew it in the fifties and the sixties.

The figures are already there, and while they may need to be taken with just as large a pinch of salt as all other officially amalgamated figures about employment in today's conditions, they are probably no more unreliable, and should be no less a sound basis for policy formation, than all the other work statistics which cause such heart-searching and provoke the familiar monthly political storms when the figures for the officially registered unemployed are announced.

What the figures broadly show is that almost a quarter of the 'working population' (a definition we have already questioned in modern conditions) now work part-time. This is almost certainly a considerable under-estimate, because we can have no idea how many people work for undeclared cash (illegally) or how many genuinely work (legally) for payments which add up to less than the single person's or married woman's allowance, and therefore may not show up in the job statistics. We know that when this part-time world does come within the purview of official reckoning it produces some very striking figures indeed. For example, the Manpower Services Commission Report for 1984/85 confirms that the growth in numbers of part-time jobs is continuing at a phenomenal rate. Over 200,000 new part-time jobs were recorded in Britain in the year reported on, and this follows an estimated figure of 150,000 the year before. Most of them were taken by women seeking some form of paid work. Male employment actually declined in both 1983/84 and 1984/85.[1]

These are trends which commonsense would lead us to expect. One does not need to dress them up in terms of women's liberation or militant feminism, unless one wishes to exaggerate the position (which of course some people do). The mood of the age is towards burden-and-role-sharing between men and women, as far as is biologically and conveniently possible. It is therefore perfectly natural that millions of women should seek work, and perfectly natural that it should be part-time work, allowing room for other work at home. It is also natural that the other half of a marriage is also going to want a matching work pattern, one that leaves room for a share of 'work' at home, outside the formal sector. So this would explain at least part of the lack of buoyancy in the figures for full-time male employment.

Thus there should be no surprise at all, or dismay, that on the supply side of the equation the labour market is changing its character radically. What people are increasingly looking for are occupations which fit in with a new social pattern and with a new conception of what feels comfortable and convenient in family and household life – a spreading of the 'more-than-one-role' aspirations already noted earlier.

The official reports from the Manpower Services Commission also confirm another major trend – which again should cause no surprise, although a great deal of policy discussion seems to take place as though it did not exist. This is the trend towards a decentralisation of paid work. Work units are getting smaller. The number who are self-employed has risen in six years from 1½ million to 2.6 million in British society or ten per cent of the so-called working population. The numbers in units employing under 200 people have increased from under 30 per cent of the workforce ten years ago, to around 60 per cent today.[2] This is the age of the 'micro' business, as our look at the fast changing structure of industry and business in the last chapter has already confirmed.

In practice, this means that sub-contracting in Britain is becoming much more commonplace. Large firms are moving

1. Dept. of Employment, 1985.
2. Census of Production Figures. Does not include agriculture.

heaven and earth to get work out of the central complex and to avoid the sort of physical concentrations of workers which in the past have always spelt awkward human relations, difficult communication problems and general management headaches at the best; foul industrial relations and embittered trade union squabbles at the worst. A sort of huge, soft bed of sub-contracting activity is now developing in Britain, pulling more and more workers out of the old formal centre. This is not the same thing as saying that there has been a 'decline in manufacturing employment'. That was always an absurd 'aggregatist' way of looking at things based on an out-of-date understanding of the way in which products are manufactured in very modern conditions. As Sarah Hogg has observed 'the statistical scale of the decline in manufacturing is misleading. It often conceals a simple switch from direct employment to contract – using a firm of accountants, say, rather than employing your own.'[1]

What is undeniable is that less and less of the manufacturing process is taking place at the 'hard' metal bashing end of the production sequence in traditional factory surroundings which orthodox economists can recongise and with which they feel familiar. Far fewer people are being herded through factory gates each morning to do heavy physical work than a decade ago. Many more people are engaged in light assembly work, service activities in support of the manufacturing process and intellectual production, all of which form a growing element in any manufactured product.

All this inevitably shows up as fewer jobs in what used to be, and is still erroneously labelled as, the manufacturing sector. But these definitions are now so blurred as to be drained of all meaning. The error is to confuse an enormously rapid change in the pattern of work with a collapse of work opportunities. That is not at all what is happening.[2]

Putting all these developments together, a work pattern emerges which is in staggering contrast with the normal one depicted in policy-making circles and political debates. On both the demand and the supply side of the labour market, the

1. *The Times*, page 17, February 20, 1984.
2. The House of Lords Select Committee on Overseas Trade, July 1985, who began their studies of the British economy from the standard definition of manufacturing, and went on to reach deeply pessimistic conclusions about Britain's production capacity clearly did not grasp the point.

requirement is increasingly for something quite different from the 'full-time' forty-eight hour-a-week factory job which most people still associate in their minds with the word 'employment'. On the demand side full-time jobs are becoming progressively rarer. On the supply side more and more people now actually prefer to work part-time for an employer, part of the time for themselves, part of the time for their families (unpaid).

The official figures cannot begin to reflect this, because they are based on a misleading and outdated definition of work. But every time one picks up a piece of the jigsaw of economic life and examines it closely there it is – a pattern which the policy makers have simply been unable to assimilate because it is so complex and varied and so far removed from the easy building blocks of debates and policy which comfortably furnished the age of aggregatist thinking. Nothing like this has ever occurred before. Perhaps there is some sort of analogy with the very early industrial pattern when cottage industries flourished before urbanisation and large scale factory operation really took hold. And perhaps there is a lesson to be gleaned from the fact that in those kind of societies and communities everyone had something to do. The general concept of unemployment simply did not exist.

But one can press the analogy with the pre-industrial revolution phase too far. People no longer live predominantly in rural communities (although there are signs that more and more would like to) and the scale of the problem is vastly greater. But the ideal of dignity, status and a role for each person is the one to hang on to. And the already emerging pattern of occupations we can now see, showing up even through the film of unreliable statistics, seems to offer a far more promising climate for achieving this ideal than the old industrialised society could ever do, even when it was operating at what was believed to be its best.

The conclusion is decisive. Full employment in the conventional sense will just not come back. The conditions which made that sort of pattern either possible or desirable have largely melted away. If the policy-makers persist in setting out as their goal a return to traditional full employment they will fail. They will do worse. They will be actively preventing the development of a far more satisfying arrangement of work and life for the vast majority than the past could ever offer.

CHAPTER 13

Income or Capital?

Astonishingly, we seem to have reached the point where, like two great river flowing together, two major trends are meeting and mixing with each other. From one direction comes the tendency in social behaviour, creating a huge new thirst for part-time work, self-employed activity, and merging paid work, unpaid work, so-called 'leisure' (which is in fact often work again), and real leisure pursuits into a new lifestyle. Flowing to meet it from another direction, there is the ever widening need in a new structure of industry and commerce for people to fit precisely these sorts of jobs. Just at the moment when people of all ages want to work increasingly in this way, industry is finding that these work patterns are precisely the ones it needs.

One can see the clash between this new alliance and the old thought modes at its clearest inside the British Labour Party – although quite a number of Conservatives, Liberals and Social Democrats seem stuck in the same tunnel. The news that part-time employment is growing extremely fast in Britain tends to be greeted with shouts of dismay and cries that these are not 'proper jobs'. In my book *Freedom and Capital* I contended that the word 'employment' itself has been the centre of much contemporary mythology in our society.[1] Over the years it has helped to freeze into a set mould a huge body of thinking about people's alleged needs and aspirations, about the shape of industry and business and about attitudes in society. I pointed out that what people really meant by 'employment' was not satisfying and useful work and occupation in all the varied forms in which it can be pursued. They meant a particular way of spending working hours in a particular kind of ambiance, in a particular kind of rhythm. Their preoccupation was almost entirely with male full-time employment. The idea embedded in their minds was that this took place in a factory or in a site

1. David Howell, *Freedom and Capital*. Blackwell 1980.

around a factory, and that it involved about forty-eight hours 'work' a week for about forty-eight weeks of the year, for about forty-eight years of a man's life, from say 17 to 65.

This was what people really meant in their heart of hearts by gainful employment. Obviously over the years, this kind of vision has had to be adjusted to take account of some awkward facts in real life – such as the growth of female employment, (which has raised by half the labour force since pre-war days), the huge expansion, indeed dominance, of service industry employment, the growth in numbers of people who want to go on working after sixty or sixty-five, and the growing army of self-employed. These are some of the exceptions which have long since overwhelmed the rule. But the essence of the idea of employment as meaning male full-time factory employment lingers on. This is what the advocates of government intervention to 'do something' about unemployment really mean when they speak of the urgent need for the government to provide more jobs. This is what really fills the thinking of Labour spokesmen when they call for more government action and this appears to be what Dr. David Owen, the S.D.P. Leader, means when he pleads for a 'deal where unions, management and government offer respectively incomes restraint, increased investment and a higher level of economic activity'.[1]

In each case there lies behind the argument a basic view that it is possible to return to the full-employment pattern of the past. Even those who recognise the enormous changes going on and welcome technological progress are inclined to interpret what they see as a repeat of the past, a shake out of jobs in one industrial sector and the growth of new full-time jobs in other sectors. What these analyses miss is that the change we are now witnessing is as much on the side of those offering work as of those creating job opportunities. Unheralded and largely unexplained, advanced societies are beginning to set themselves new goals which lie beyond the old simplicities of full employment.

The puzzle is why politicians and policy-makers continue to cling so stubbornly to the idea of employment for all as the nirvana which we must reach or to which we must return. The answer seems to lie in two ideas which are very deeply fixed. The first idea is that full-time employment, in the familiar sense,

1. Dr. David Owen *A Future that Will Work* (Penguin) page 15.

is the only conceivable way of providing a means of existence, that it is synonymous with income – and therefore spending and living standards. The second idea is that the alternative to employment is idleness, that employment is the one and only means of ensuring that people have a minimum of human dignity and status. Work without pay, this argument goes, is work without dignity. Part-time work therefore must be inferior to a full-time job and the growth of part-time employment must involve both an attack on living standards and on human dignity.

We have here what is called the 'wage mentality'. Because it is assumed that wages determine purchasing power and living standards and because it is assumed that wages come from full-time employment, then it must follow that full-time remunerated employment is a moral necessity for all, an essential goal of public policy. The addendum to this argument is that since wages are everything then if society is to be fairer it is wage differentials which must be operated upon. Similarly, if inflation is to be curbed without devastating unemployment, or if other policy goals are to be achieved in this area, then again it is pay, identifiable wages and salaries, which must somehow be levelled, frozen or otherwise influenced. As we saw in Section II, this has become the orthodox 'Keynesian' position. The cruder the macro-economic controls, the more the need to control incomes, and by extension, prices, direct. Of course those who think in this 'wages' mode have to concede that at the margin there may be people for whom pay and work are quite separate. They recognise that there is a rentier class who live off capital as well as a class for whom income from work is so miserably low that it is supplemented by other 'income' – in this case from state benefits.

It is often the case where beliefs are very well established and very widely held about the general state of society that they continue to carry great weight long after they have ceased to be generally true. The exception to some general proposition about how people live and behave may far outweigh the numbers who fit the rule. Yet somehow the conventional wisdom lives on like a thin pie crust from which the pie beneath has long since been removed. The general rule continues to assert that income comes from paid work. The facts are quite different. The family which relies on one income from one paid job is now probably the exception rather than the rule in our society. The statistical model of the single bread winner bringing home from his job the wherewithal to maintain family living standards is actually becoming appropriate only to a minority. In 1985 there were only 48 per cent of households in which husband and wife were both of working age, which conformed to this model.[1] In all the rest both partners worked, either part-time or full-time. Figures for 1984 also show that 7 million households received income from sources outside their regular paid work – either from additional small jobs or from investments.[2] These figures grossly under-estimate the pattern, in fact they are bound to do so since they cannot take account of the black economy incomes. More reliable figures confirm that 7 million households were also in 1984 drawing child benefit,[3] additional income coming from outside the remunerated wage pattern.

Sources of Support
This, of course, is only a tiny corner of a much larger, indeed a gargantuan spread of state benefits, involving the gathering and redistribution of some £40 billion annually in Britain. It is helpful to see how this huge flow of income, in many cases a supplementary or second income, fits into the new world of work and activity we have been describing. The answer is, very messily, and in a way which, not surprisingly, is very hostile to the emergence of new and more flexible work patterns. Almost all state payments taper off as earnings increase from work of any sort (so long as it is declared). Even the state retirement pension, which one would expect to be an unconditional state income payment, is reduced for those up to seventy who are still earning above a specified amount (currently £75) under the iniquitous earnings rule.

The disincentive to those who would like to add earnings to their basic state benefits is therefore strong. When one includes the additional effect of rising marginal tax rates the discouragement to paid work, part-time or full-time, is devastating. It has been calculated that over the range of £60 a week to £130 a week it does not pay a married man with two children to increase earnings at all. Just about the only incomes which are currently insulated from the levels of paid work activity are

1. Annual Abstract of Statistics. Add in couples over official 'working age' and of course the percentage is much lower still.
2. National Income Blue Book.
3. PEWP 1986.

child credits, which are a sort of left-over from a past abortive attempt at comprehensive social security and tax reform, and Enterprise Allowance scheme, under which people may draw unemployment pay while starting up on their own in business. Even here the Inland Revenue have devised a system for taxing the Enterprise Allowance in a way which rapidly erodes its incentive value.[1]

All this has led one school of thought to argue for a simple and satisfying solution. This would be to provide a guaranteed and *unconditional* basic income for all who have left full-time schooling, whether they worked full-time, part-time, stayed at home or had no sort of occupation at all. This scheme would involve the total overthrow of the original Beveridge principle of benefits tailored to the requirements of those 'in need'. The beauty of it is that it makes the labour market vastly more flexible. The whole focus of government attempts to ensure adequate living standards for all would shift away from efforts to rig the labour market by complex wages legislation, or to devise desperate job-preservation schemes at vast cost, since the guaranteed basic income would take care of all that. People would be free, or freer at any rate, to accept low-wage and part-time jobs. The unemployed would no longer be discouraged from taking some work to top up their basic income. The temptation to join the black economy and work for undeclared income so as to protect state benefits would evaporate.

If the retirement pension was also re-designated as a guaranteed basic income, then the horrors of the earnings rule would go. More fundamentally, the whole idea of a retirement pension, and of a fixed national retirement age, at which people stopped contributing and became dependants, would begin to be eroded. This would fit in not only with a much more flexible work pattern but with the growing idea that the ages of sixty or sixty-five are now obsolete as dividing lines between middle and old age and that people now remain vigorous and eager to work, on average, for much longer than in the past, often well into their seventies. Indeed, we all know octogenarians of amazing vigour who can probably work as effectively as people half their age.

The unconditional basic income idea would also help solve the dilemma for mothers or fathers with young children. Their

1. Now put right in the 1986 Budget.

basic income would continue whether they stayed at home or went out to work, part-time or full-time. The incentive for both partners to go out to work at the same time would, of course, be greatly reduced. But there are two huge snags to this idea of total insulation of state benefits from status or need.

The first is that while the incentive to earn more would increase, or to work for low pay or no pay in the community, so would the incentive for many to be completely and anti-socially idle. 'Why Work?' would become an even more tempting question than under the present range of discouragements.

The second and much bigger snag is that a system of guaranteed basic incomes for all would be colossally expensive and involve impossibly high tax rates. Even when one takes into account the £8 billion of benefits now going to the unemployed, which would be part of the new basic income scheme, and the savings on existing benefit and job-support schemes, and the switch of all the resources now going into paying people's state pensions, the tax rates required to provide a basic income on which all could live at an acceptable minimum level would be self-defeatingly high. For these reasons, some other ideas which seek to be equally comprehensive in place of the present mishmash have been put forward.

Ralph Howell MP has proposed a universal Right to Work scheme.[1] Under this scheme unemployment benefits would cease after three or six months. All people over sixteen would then have the right to work, the work to be made available through Work Centres throughout the country who would organise a huge system of employment, mostly in upgrading the environment. Pay would rise up to a maximum for adults of £80 a week. This, he believes, would abolish involuntary unemployment.

But the trouble with both this approach, as well as with the idea of a guaranteed basic income is that they both create great armies of dependants on state initiative in an age when that is decreasingly desired or necessary. It may be argued that they offer a more orderly and less negative kind of dependance than the present haphazard and labyrinthine benefit arrangements, which in an odd and unfair way already channel partial 'basic incomes' of various sorts to everyone already. But society is now trying to move in quite a different direction. People are

1. *Why Unemployment?* by Ralph Howell M.P. Adam Smith Institute 1985.

seeking less dependence, less centralisation and more personal control over their lives and work. The policy-makers ought therefore to be looking for ways of reducing reliance on gigantic central state schemes of welfare, make-work and income support altogether. It should become an open aim of social policy to do away with the inefficiencies, the insensitivities and the inadequacies of the centrally administered welfare state.

The best path for the policy-makers should therefore probably be to begin with unconditionality on a limited scale – limited both in size of basic income paid and by income level of the recipient (except in old age), but to combine this with policies to open up new sources of support for living standards. This will admittedly still leave us with the existing problem of disincentives to take work and with the inescapable problem of a disincentive operating at the point, whether tapered or abrupt, at which income support ceases to be the automatic entitlement. Possibly a partial version of the Ralph Howell scheme might work. Part of the existing flow of income going to those who are unemployed could be made available unconditionally and designated as the basic income, and part would be paid as a top-up in exchange for work to which all would have access under the Right to Work law.

This would be a slightly less messy but still very unsatisfactory pattern, leaving millions of people still heavily dependent on the creaking central state and its agencies for their purchasing power and living standards. That is why the need is to move policy-thinking sideways out of its overwhelming preoccupation with weekly incomes and 'wages', whether from the state or from the employer, and to bring the concept of personal ownership to the centre of the scene. A massive banking up of personal capital resources for families in all income groups is a perfectly feasible goal. If achieved on a sufficient scale it would provide precisely the same consequential and highly beneficial effects as those claimed for the inordinately expensive idea of a guaranteed basic income for all. That is to say, it would give people of all ages more freedom to work for low pay or on a voluntary basis. It would open out possibilities for both enterprise, work and welfare to be organised on a far more local and intimate scale than the huge welfare state system has been able to provide. It would open the way for a much freer and more flexible labour market.

These ideas and prospects will be filled out in the next

chapter. But in the meantime it should be noted that all moves towards the divorce of income and living standards considerations from concern about employment, whether through an unconditional basic income scheme or through 'capital' bonuses supplementing basic pay, or through wider capital ownership, will have a wholly beneficial effect both on the state of thinking at central government level about economic and social policy and on attitudes to pay, productivity and jobs at the level of the shop floor.

The 'wage' obsession has now bedevilled and distorted policy thinking in Britain for three decades. The state of mind persists in policy-making circles, in Whitehall, in policy research organisations and in all the political parties even while everyday practice and reality are already diverging in a wholly different direction, despite a hostile policy climate and despite the lack of policy schemes or strategies of the sort discussed above. As the figures increasingly confirm, we have reached the stage when a large minority of the population, possibly even a majority, find that income from their main job is only one element in supporting their living standards and that income from the state, income from capital, or capital spent directly, or income from a second job, or services received in exchange for services given on a barter basis, form an increasing part of the system by which a family supports its living standards.

What is new is the scale rather than the trend. The illusion that people's visible incomes determined their living standards was precisely the one that Nicholas Kaldor sought to destroy in his book *An Expenditure Tax* published almost thirty years ago.[1] The central contention in *An Expenditure Tax* was that the gap between spending power and visible taxable earned wages and salaries was large and growing larger for a growing number of families. It was Nicky Kaldor's belief that a fair and honest taxation system should take account of this. Since Kaldor was and remains a strong egalitarian he believes that very intense account of this factor should be taken indeed in tax policy. But his starting point was and is valid for policy-making whatever the political prejudice – namely that earned income – i.e. wages – are only a partial determinant of living standards.

This process of divergence has continued and is bound to go very much further, as high technology increases the rewards of

1. Nicholas Kaldor *An Expenditure Tax* George Allen and Unwin 1955.

capital and weakens the demand for unskilled labour. The general proposition that pay from a full-time job determines living standards, and that all must be slotted into full-time jobs, is crumbling before our eyes. Attention will have to be increasingly turned to the wider distribution of non-wage resources, notably capital and income from capital, if any conceivable sense of unity and common purpose, embracing the whole of modern industrial society, is to be re-created.

In the next chapter we shall see how this can in practice be done. In the meantime, for those who believe that the idea of spreading capital resources so widely that all families can benefit is fantasy, it is perhaps worth reflecting that in Britain there are now 3 million owner-occupied homes in the hands of people over sixty on which the mortgage has been paid off. Since the current average house price is £30,000, the children of this generation over the next twenty-five years – who will also already own homes – will inherit about £90 billion worth of assets transforming and spreading the pattern of capital owner-ship to a far greater extent than would have been believed possible even a decade ago.[1]

It is through the 'wages' preoccupation and the continuing blindness towards questions of capital distribution and owner-ship, that policy makers have been led repeatedly up the cul-de-sac of incomes policy. The conviction that income from paid work is the only available reward and must be the key determi-nant of living standards has led a whole generation of politicians to the apparently unsinkable view that wages and salaries must somehow be centrally controlled. There is a double blindness here. What is controlled must first be identified so that the policy-makers know, at least in some crude way, what they are supposed to be controlling. The difficulties which post war governments have experienced in trying to identify people's true income and then administer 'fair' or unfair controls over them have been formidable enough. Successive deals, announced with great fanfares, between central government and the unions have turned out to be, in the words of Joel Barnett, the Labour Chief Secretary in the seventies, 'all take and no give'.[2] The unions have not been able to deliver. Even where nationally identified and negotiated wage rates have

1. Estimate given in ABM.
2. Joel Barnett: *Inside the Treasury.* André Deutsch, 1982.

responded to central influence, down at the grass roots in the real world, all kinds of local and individual arrangements, at the plant and in the small enterprise, have succeeded in making the figures meaningless.

But even these problems pale into insignificance as the soft, dispersed economy replaces the old industrial model, and information about incomes which was vague and misleading enough before, becomes many times more so in the new condition. The reality is that even if income from labour were still the best guide to wealth distribution in society, the means available to central government to influence the pattern directly have now broken down beyond repair. Only those quite oblivious of the now wholly changed nature of work and industry and the labour market could continue to press for central policies to control wages and salaries. It may well be a dim realisation of these formidable problems which have led the advocates of incomes policy – who tend to belong in the United Kingdom to what are misleadingly labelled the 'moderate' and 'middle way' schools of economics – to re-think their position and argue instead for tax policies which would somehow influence wage negotiations.

Particularly strong support has been forthcoming for Professor James Meade's ideas and Professor Richard Layard's proposals for taxing wages granted above a certain norm, which we examine in Chapter 16. Yet even here, and even if incomes were still the right target to be controlled, getting the correct information about settlements in an increasingly dispersed pattern of economic activity, with a rapidly growing informal sector, would be a task which, if difficult in earliest times, is now probably completely impossible. The strongest sounding enthusiasts for a return to these nostrums tend, when it comes to the detail of how they would work, to become studiously vague. Thus Dr. David Owen, a firm prisoner of out-dated thinking on incomes, boldly calls for 'some form of incomes policy' as the *sine qua non* of successful economic management by central government. Under pressure this becomes modified to 'a viable incomes policy ready to use if necessary,' and this in turn melts into 'a decentralised and flexible incomes strategy which is not susceptible to a national formula'. Finally, like the fading grin of the Cheshire Cat, the whole idea dwindles in Dr. Owen's hands into the rueful acknowledgement that the more decentralised pattern of negotiating required 'cannot however be quickly or easily achieved'. The Owen prescription then finally slides off into some unexceptionable proposals for reforming arbitration procedures and to the call for an inflation tax as a reserve power on the Statute Book.

Firms that wish to pay increases above the norm (to be worked out in ways undefined) would have the choice either of distributing the extra in shares (a tiny brush here with the new reality – just a glimpse beyond the curtain) or pay the tax. Somehow, this is supposed to form the basis of a deal between unions, management and government.[1] In practice it would do no such thing, even if there were paper agreement for a brief while, for the simple reason that the scheme could only catch 'visible' wages and salaries. And society would quickly recognise this as intolerably unfair. But even if the wildly improbable occurred and some influence was achieved on visible and recorded wages and salaries, mostly those which had been nationally negotiated, the central question would remain – is this really the main issue? Or should the focus be much less on wage and salary incomes and much more on capital? Should the concern be much less with seeking to identify and restrain individual incomes and much more on ways of turning income into capital and expanding personal capital holdings? The thought seems to have come to a whole generation of 'income' specialists and experts in the procedures by which wages and salaries are settled, painfully and slowly. Yet at root it is a very simple one. The more that a family's or an individual's living standards can be built on capital resources, or at least on capital bonuses over and above basic pay, and the smaller the significance of the weekly wage in financing the overall living standard, the readier people will be to work in a pattern which gives them the most satisfaction throughout the week and to mix their paid work with voluntary work or part paid work in the informal sector in a form which benefits the community and enhances individual independence and dignity.

That this is already happening on a very wide scale in our society is beyond dispute. That it coincides with both a natural desire for both partners in a marriage to have a more satisfying and balanced part of life outside the home as well as inside the home, is also now very clear and fully confirmed by the statistics. That the structure of industry and employment are now

---

1. Dr. David Owen *A Future that will Work*, pp. 12ff (Penguin 1984).

altering very fast in a way which fits precisely with these new aspirations is also becoming evident. The obvious cushion on which these work and life patterns will have to rest, if they are to be consistent with a high standard of living for all, is widespread capital ownership. One would have expected all policymakers and political leaders of the right and in the centre of the political spectrum, and even some collectivists as well, to accept the clear desirability of these arrangements. If the mechanism of wage bargaining is the heart of the problem, that is where one would expect reforming effort to concentrate.

Yet that has not been the case at all. Although the conditions are becoming increasingly appropriate for the emergence of a society enjoying widespread capital ownership and shaping its attitudes and behaviour on such a pattern, although the ideal of fair shares for all through the mechanism of employment for all has now clearly passed beyond reach for good, and although a new settlement is visibly coming into being which gives far more prominence and importance to capital ownership, the idea that we might have here the ingredients of a new social order and a new goal to replace the full employment ideal of the post war decades has been pitifully slow to catch on. It is to this strange state of affairs, this historic failure of imagination by the policy-makers that we now turn.

PART V

Capitalism and Social Progress

'A democracy is a polity in which it is possible to participate as citizens, so Capitalism is an economy in which it is possible for all men to participate as capitalists.'

Louis Kelso, *The Capitalist Manifesto*

CHAPTER 14

Wider Ownership: The Absolutely Central Goal

The Ignored Ideal

The idea of wider personal ownership as the central goal of social policy has been persistently advanced over the years by a handful of politicians and one or two economists, and persistently ignored by almost everyone else. In particular, the academic and intellectual establishment has paid almost no attention at all to the wider ownership idea or its implications for the structure of society or the role of government. For example, the Fontana Dictionary of Modern Thought has no entry under either property or ownership, although it carries substantial references to Labour's defunct social compact, to social democracy, social engineering, participation, productivity bargaining and the Provos. Profit sharing gets a brief mention.[1] Yet the notion of widespread personal ownership as an antidote to collectivism and as an obvious escape route from the class war between wages and capital is far from new. In the thirties Anthony Eden was making speeches about the need for a property-owning democracy. In the forties both Conservative and Liberal leaders in Britain strongly supported a variety of wider ownership ideas.

Then in the late fifties a book was published in America of dazzling prescience explaining how a socialised society needed to be replaced, and in due course would be replaced, by a social order based on greatly broadened individual ownership, both of private enterprise and of public utilities and other undertakings. The book, The Capitalist Manifesto, was written by Louis Kelso and appeared in 1958.[2] In the high noon of post-war Keynesianism in Europe it received virtually no recognition at

1. Fontana/Collins 1977.
2. Random House, 1958.

all. Yet Kelso believed deeply that mass ownership of industry and enterprise offered by far the best way out of the Keynesian inflationary ambush, as he described it (which he had correctly diagnosed as the likely post-war consequence of over enthusiastic attempts by central government to manipulate aggregate demand). He attacked Keynes not for his perfectly sensible ideas for expanding public works and running a budget deficit in a depression, but for surrendering on the wages front, for assuming that money wages and salaries could not and would not be flexible downwards and that union power would never permit downward adjustment. He argued that Keynes had ignored the most promising way out of the inflation-versus-full-employment dilemma, by neglecting the enormous potential of the wider capital ownership idea. Why, he asked, should not high living standards for all, *and* mass purchasing power, be maintained both via income from labour *and* income from capital resources. The best hope, he urged, for the non-socialist future lay with policies for wider capital ownership. This was surely the right route to dignity and status for all in a stable and unified society, the way to an economic as well as a political democracy. Kelso proposed a number of detailed schemes for greatly widening both employee share ownership in private enterprises and ownership of shares in public utilities as well. He made a proposal, dismissed at the time as ridiculous fantasy, that consumers of services provided by public utilities should be converted into shareholders. A quarter of a century later, this is of course precisely what has happened in the case of British Telecom.

In fact, Keynes himself was not totally unaware of the wider capital ownership argument. In *How to Pay for the War* Keynes suggested that the answer to inflationary pressure from excess wage demands might be through the distribution of shares to workers. So Keynes certainly saw the dangers coming. But Louis Kelso was quite right that the post-war Keynesians had forgotten all about this. Indeed, the thought does not seem to have entered into their writing or policy recommendation at any stage at all.

Miniature Capitalism
In preparing our ideas inside the Conservative Party in opposition, between 1964 and 1970, we sought to build on the Kelso

insights and to broaden the whole idea of a widespread personal capital ownership into the major Conservative theme. It seemed to some of us to offer the obvious way forward on both the economic and social fronts. We saw wider ownership as synonymous with encouragement for smaller enterprises and with a general renaissance of the smaller, more flexible, less controlled side of British industry and commerce. We saw in wider individual ownership policies the opportunity to reduce the huge concentrations of power which had accumulated in the nationalised industries and services. And we saw the opportunity to redress the balance between private economic influence and the growing domination of the giant financial institutions. Above all, we believed that the spread of capital ownership to as many families and individuals as possible opened the way to a lessening in people's dependence as employees and nothing else. It meant the spread of personal dignity and individual status and a general rolling back of the rule of officialdom, with its master servant connotation which we found so unpleasant and in which we saw a sinister future, as Orwell had done before us. More personal ownership meant in effect the miniaturisation of capital in line with the miniaturisation of the industrial structure.

It has to be said that the climate for these ideas after 1970, when the Conservatives had been returned to office, remained extremely negative and hostile. Commentators and columnists were not really interested, being far more preoccupied with the intricacies of incomes policy and with 'macro-economic' solutions to the major problems of society, as we saw in Chapters 2 and 5. Industrialists thought people were 'not ready' for popular, or 'miniature', capitalism. Policy makers felt that the whole body of thought might make good speech material but was marginal to the main dilemmas the nation faced.

I remember one particularly dispiriting visit to the late Sir John Methven, Director General of the CBI, to discuss the wider ownership theme. Sir John, who had an open mind and an enthusiastic approach to economic reform, had to warn me that his members would only be politely interested in the idea of wider ownership of shares for employees, no more, and would be positively hostile to any strong government policies aimed at promoting really widespread share ownership by workers. Employers would regard all this, he explained, as a dangerous distraction. Capital was for shareholders and wages were for workers. So much for equality of opportunity and of economic status in our society!

Today things do indeed seem to be different. There is a much less patronising attitude towards worker capitalism. Industrialists predict and welcome the trend towards people going into business on their own account as mini-capitalists. It is estimated that there are now more than 1000 medium-sized or large firms with employee share ownership schemes, covering three quarters of a million workers. Speeches from senior Ministers are again full of pledges to build the capital owning democracy and truly popularise capitalism. The Prime Minister, Mrs Thatcher, has described the extension of property ownership more and more widely as 'the historic task of all governments that love liberty'.[1] The Chancellor of the Exchequer, Nigel Lawson, has repeatedly and vigorously supported the theme as providing the best way forward in a non-socialist environment. It was a major feature of the 1986 Budget statement. Distinguished economic commentators, too, notably Samuel Brittan writing in the *Financial Times*, have warmly embraced the whole concept of a fairer distribution of capital ownership as being part of the answer to a perplexing situation in which market clearing wages could, for many people, turn out to be below the level needed to provide decent living standards. All this is none the less welcome for coming regrettably late in the day. In fact it suggests that shafts of reality are beginning to break through the low grey cloud base of the British political debate.

Flaws in the Tapestry
On the Conservative side the process has been vastly helped by the realisation that other strands of policy – the revival of the small business sector and the push for privatisation of state assets – are all potentially part of the same unfolding tapestry. I say 'potentially' because in 1979 the Treasury did not understand this point or, if it did, it was not very interested in it. For the shapers of economic policy in the Treasury privatisation was all to do with raising cash and improving the look of the government's borrowing requirement, to the precise size of which was attached enormous (and wholly unrealistic) psychological importance. This attitude still lingers in parts of the

1. At the Mansion House Lord Mayor's Banquet, November 1983.

Treasury and could yet inflict further damage on the otherwise hearteningly vigorous programme of privatisation and dispersal of previously narrowly held assets in state industry.

One piece of good fortune in the mid eighties in Britain is that there has now come to the Treasury a new Financial Secretary, John Moore, who grasps the wider implication of privatisation and the place of the policy within the context of overall social aims, very clearly indeed. His task and that of other Treasury Ministers will now be to see that the enormous privatisation programme, as it proceeds on its way, is conducted with increasing emphasis on the goal of a widespread equity ownership, even where this reduces the proceeds to the Treasury, and the immediate gains to the Public Sector Borrowing Requirement, below what they might otherwise be.

Meanwhile, Samuel Brittan has characteristically gone into the issue very deeply indeed and has made the intellectual connection which many of us were urging a decade ago, between capital distribution and the wages issue. But whereas our hope and contention in a previous decade was that wider capital distribution would moderate ceaseless demands for inflationary wage increases, Brittan has focussed on the contemporary problem of mass unemployment. The argument goes like this: if major inroads are to be made into unemployment and some kind of satisfying occupation provided for all, then this will only occur if wages are truly flexible (i.e. if job seekers are prepared to accept lower rates or work for shorter hours – despite Keynes's insistence that this would not happen). In consequence, more people may have to work for worse remuneration which could fall short of what is required for a minimum decent standard of living, as determined by contemporary standards.

Up to this point Samuel Brittan, and others who take the same view about flexible wage rates, are only saying what classical economists like Professor Pigou always said – namely that the path to a full pattern of employment lies primarily not through the 'bellows' approach of demand expansion, monetary or fiscal, by central government action but through allowing wages to be adjusted at levels which clear the labour market. But here Mr Brittan takes the leap which neither market-economist monetarists, nor traditional Keynesians, have been ready to take. If the wages at which jobs for all become available are indeed found to be below the levels needed for a decent stan-

dard of living, what is the answer? On the one hand there is
the Keynesian response, which is that they should not be
offered and will not be accepted. 'Workers' wrote Keynes in
The General Theory, 'will usually resist a reduction in money
wages' and he argued that it was a very good thing they did.
The 'answer' lay through fiscal and monetary manipulation at
the macro-economic level.[1]

On the other hand, the classical economists argue that a low
wage is better than no wage (which of course is not in fact the
case under existing social security provisions or with the kind
of unemployment pay levels that are generally regarded as
adequate and just).

The Third Approach
But there is a third approach and it is one that has been deftly
grasped by Mr Brittan. It is to seek to compensate, as far as
possible through capital distribution, for what the employment
market mechanism can no longer provide through conventional
wages and salaries. It is to allow the market for wages to work
while encouraging genuine equality of status and circumstance
through widespread personal capital accumulation.

'Why is this so terrible a prospect?' asks Mr Brittan. 'A shift
in market rewards away from labour towards capital is a disaster
only if capital is highly concentrated and many workers have
very little except for a stake in their own houses. If, however,
income-earning assets were to be so widely distributed that
every family derived a substantial annual amount from them,
market clearing wages would become once more a political
possibility; and the pressure for measures such as job-sharing
to reduce the supply of labour would be somewhat less.'[2]

It would be more than a possibility. It would be a reinforcement of a trend which society seems eager and ready to accept,
indeed which has already begun. For what are those who take
part-time jobs for part-time wages in their millions doing if they
are not voting for precisely this new kind of pattern? And what
are those in industry and commerce doing as they design and
develop new processes and procedures which work best on the
basis of part-time labour or sub-contracted operations, if they

1. Page 9.
2. From 'The Politics and Economics of Privatisation', *Political Quarterly*, April
   1974.

are not creating precisely the conditions in which labour demand and supply fit comfortably together in a way which is not only possible but highly desirable?

In practice, the shift away from formal work and wage structures, and towards a more personalised work pattern is already very much under way. For example, self-employment is growing at a great pace. There is an enormous surge of interest in almost every part of Britain – even including the allegedly 'dead' inner city areas – in small enterprise, how to get it going, how to be part of it, how in short to escape the deadweight of wage dependence. Every magazine stand is now jammed with publications offering advice on getting a small enterprise up and running and overcoming all the teething problems. 'Starting your own business' has long since ceased to be an impossible dream and became the subject of the most normal everyday discussion. Local authorities and Chambers of Commerce have formed agencies across the nation to give counsel, help, warning, instruction and guidance to people of all ages who want to start up business of all kinds *and are quite prepared to accept low incomes while doing so.* Sleepy clearing banks are beginning to be less downright discouraging towards the would-be entrepreneur who at the outset has nothing but self-confidence and a few savings as security. Indeed the starter may not even have that. Government initiatives like the imaginative Enterprise Allowance Scheme, which helps unemployed people to start up on their own, fit into the very heart of this new scheme. So do several other central and locally inspired schemes – including some initiated by larger private sector undertakings – which give individual wage and salary earners the access to funds, the encouragement and the guidance they need to launch out into an independent environment.

Yet, despite all this ferment, so long as government policy and public debate focus *only* on wages and salaries, the capital side of the equation is bound to remain needlessly obscure. It is as though half the full policy picture has been left out. And half a policy, like a chair with two legs, does not stand up. This explains why frequent Ministerial appeals both for incomes restraint and for lower wage rates, so that more people can be employed, tend to please logicians and economists but displease general opinion mightily. General opinion is right and the economists are wrong. The missing half of the proposition, from which talk of more flexible wages should never be disconnected, is that in a liberal and decentralised society, where the work opportunities are endless and where there is always plenty of work of some kind to be done, support for a decent living standard must be expected to come not just from wages but from capital sources as well. The opening up and vigorous development of these capital sources, as a vital additional prop to family living standards, is just as much part of the necessary labour market reform as are all the other proposals for increased wage flexibility and for lifting the burdens that prevent the labour market working.

This is the point at which the ideal of wider ownership becomes not just another piece of anti-socialist and anti-collectivist rhetoric, *but the key to the solution of the Keynesian dilemma, the successor idea to the Keynesian economic and political order*. Yet curiously it is a key which some monetarist have just not been able to grasp or turn in the lock.

Monetarism, Professor Brian Griffiths, the new head of the Prime Minister's Policy Unit at No 10 has explained to us, is intended to remove the monetary causes of inflation. 'It was not designed to solve the problem of long-term structural unemployment'. That is a matter of major labour market reform.[1] (CPS Summer Address, 1985). Very much the same message comes to us from the Chancellor of the Exchequer, Nigel Lawson, in his Mais Lecture, 'The British Experiment'.[2] 'It is the conquest of inflation' Mr Lawson argues, 'and not the pursuit of growth and employment, which is or should be the objective of macro-economic policy. And it is the creation of conditions conducive to growth and employment, and not the suppression of price rises, which is or should be the objective of micro-economic policy.' 'Relatively free markets', he continues, 'the spirit of enterprise and workers who prefer to price themselves into jobs, rather than out of them, are a powerful engine of employment.'

Yet it is this 'powerful engine' which Keynes thought would not function, for the very good and liberal reason that he did not see either the trades unions, or society generally, tolerating the lower living standards which he thought – and many still assume – are inevitably implied by lower wage rates. Every time the monetarist zealots call for more flexible labour markets,

1. Centre for Policy Studies, Summer Address 1985.
2. Delivered to the Centre for International Banking and Finance, June 1984.

they sound as though this is precisely what they *would* tolerate – and are then surprised and hurt at the total and utter political and social unacceptability of their message.

Unravelling the Dilemma
The capital ownership dimension begins to unravel this dilemma. It changes the terms on which rewards are negotiated. It permits governments to commit themselves to a genuinely cohesive social policy and to a degree of genuine equality of status in society, which they can no longer credibly promise to deliver through committing themselves to full employment in the old sense of providing full-time life-time jobs for all.

It is true that since 1979 the Conservatives in Britain have in practice taken a considerable number of steps towards widening of personal ownership and creating precisely the conditions in which less dependence on full-time wage can become genuinely consistent with good living standards. In the six years since 1979 home ownership has been considerably extended (from 53% to 62% of the population). Meanwhile, the privatisation programme continues to enlarge the number of individual shareholders and has brought several hundred thousand additional employees into the shareholding community. If it succeeds, the sale of British Gas to the public could add at least another million first-time equity shareholders to the 'new' million who hold British Telecom shares.

On the pension front, steps have been taken or are planned which are equally significant for wider ownership. Personal occupational pension schemes for those with incomes from non-pensionable employment – i.e. the self-employed or part self-employed – have been given enormous encouragement. Some help has been given to those who want to take their pensions with them from job to job and the pressure is now on for measures to allow members of existing pension schemes generally to switch to personal portable pensions. A move of this kind of course strikes a double blow for wider personal ownership – both by individualising ownership at present held collectively in the pension funds and by creating a far greater sense of direct involvement and ownership in the minds of the pension beneficiary. All these are moves of a highly liberating kind.

They reduce wage dependence and enlarge personal economic freedom in a direct and positive way.[1]

So why, then, do governments, including the present British one, remain so much on the defensive about pay, jobs and work? It can only be because they are still looking at pieces of a jigsaw without a picture and without a frame. Except in the case of home ownership, and in particular the opportunities created for former council tenants to purchase the houses in which they already lived, all these measures, and the attitudes they foster, still really only apply to a limited minority. Even now, after the spectacular sale of British Telecom shares already mentioned, the number of individual owners of equity shares in Britain is probably little over three million – 6% of the population of the United Kingdom. If Britain is to continue pioneering social reform based on wider individual ownership, then it still has a very long way to go even to catch up with the levels of personal ownership in neighbouring European societies, let alone in the United States of America where the equivalent figure is 25%.

Even worse from the point of view of the cause of wider ownership has been the inexorable growth in the proportion of total registered wealth, other than home, in the hands of pension funds and other financial institutions. In the years ahead, this may be gradually checked by greater incentives to people to own their own pension plans and possibly by the marginal reforms now proposed for the State Earnings Related Pension Scheme. But all this will take a very long time. No one can be entirely sure about the extent to which these changes will truly result in the personalisation of ownership and in a real growth in a sense of personal involvement which direct ownership should bring.

All in all, rhetoric has tended to reach well ahead of actual progress in widening capital ownership and in establishing on a really widespread scale, the strong senses of both personal responsibility and obligation, and of belonging to and sharing in a society as a whole, that ought to go with it.

---

1. These moves have now been supplemented by a new scheme proposed in the 1986 Budget for relieving tax on the income from small savings when invested in equities – the so-called Personal Equity Plan.

The Real Test

So the real test now is whether the rhetoricians are prepared to move on from generalities to decisive measures, whether policy makers are really prepared to challenge not just the state-owned concentration of wealth but the huge wealth concentrations which have grown up elsewhere as well: whether, in short, they are prepared to wrench themselves away from their obsession with income distribution and with traditional ideas about employment as the only valid form of work, and instead start promoting the truly capitalist revolution.

What does that involve? For one thing, it certainly means a much more vigorous refusal than hitherto evident, to be overwhelmed by the dominance of financial institutions. At the very least, one would expect to see moves to equalise the fiscal advantages between individual savers and institutions, in a way that most certainly does not yet exist on the British fiscal scene.

Philip Chappell, of Morgan Grenfell, the bankers, has forcefully argued that the guiding principles in this area should be fiscal equality. By this he means, I think, something rather different from, and possibly more practical than, fiscal neutrality, which at one stage appeared to be the cause to which the Conservative tax reformers had attached their colours. By fiscal equality, Mr Chappell means that there should be a pattern of tax incentives which are as favourable to personal savings as to savings through institutions. Along with Nigel Vinson, another veteran campaigner for wider ownership, Mr Chappell has proposed a plan for allowing all individuals to set aside any part of their annual income and place it in a segregated personal investment pool.[1] It would enter this pool free of all tax. Income tax liability would only arise when savings from the pool were withdrawn. As Chappell and Vinson point out, even this would not provide true fiscal equality with pension fund arrangements, where the additional tax privilege exists of commutation and the extraction of a lump sum tax free. But it would be a major step in the right direction.

There is another area of ownership too, in which a wider spread has yet to be positively encouraged – and that is on the land. We will need to see policies which at least ceased to

1. See 'Owners All' A proposal for Personal Investment Pools, by Philip Chappell and Nigel Vinson, Centre for Policy Studies, October 1985.

encourage larger and larger scale production and concentration of land holding, and at best promoted dispersal.

At the moment, these are patently not the agricultural and land policies in place in Britain. As we saw in Chapter 7, the statistics of land holdings show a remorseless amalgamation of acreages into even larger units and a steady decline in the number owning or farming land. Clearly, the historic task of the Conservatives to widen the ownership of property has not yet reached the ears of the agricultural policy makers or the guardians of the traditional landed interest.

Then, third, if popular ownership and a significant spread of economic power really are the social aims in our society, the decision to move large public monopolies into the private sector with their powers virtually intact, and with only a veneer of regulations, raises some severe question marks, to put it at its mildest. British Telecom, and the British Gas Corporation, may become, as we have noted, much more widely owned after privatisation than when they were under Whitehall's control. But to what extent has a real dispersal of economic power (or indeed any real increase in competition) in practice been achieved by these transfers? The danger is that if people feel that wider ownership is some kind of trick – a device to keep the workers quiet while power remains as tightly concentrated in monopoly hands as ever, then the collectivist opponents of the wider ownership idea will have an easy opportunity to discredit the whole movement and all its supporting policies.

The reality is that the various measures and changes undertaken have not really yet engendered a mass change of attitude or the creation of a different culture throughout society which might help to eliminate the 'wages' and 'them-against-us' mentalities of the past. Nor is this very surprising when one sees how timid the challenge has been against the great wealth-holding concentrations and interests. The impulses are there, as we have seen, towards owning as well as earning, towards more independent work patterns, towards a world in which employment is no longer regarded as the only valid form of work, or income from employment as the only valid source of livelihood. But all the supporting policies are not yet in place.

CHAPTER 15

Ownership and Care

We have seen that the idea of ownership of wealth as a popular entitlement, as a normal social condition, has not yet really begun to march. Nor, except in a partial way, have the attitudes taken hold in popular consciousness which should go with a society in which it was normal for most people to act and think like owners as well as earners. Had they done so, I believe we would have seen a very much faster and larger change than has in fact been the case in habitual ways of thinking and in the centralist ideas which still dominate the minds of the policy-makers and politicians.

First, we would have seen a far more positive and popular connection established between the culture of widespread ownership and the ideals of care and concern for the under-occupied, the disadvantaged and the most vulnerable members of any community. The belief that 'the state will look after' (meaning that nobody else need really bother) would have been far more rapidly discredited than has proved the case so far.

Second, we might have seen the realisation grow that extended individual ownership goes far to provide the answer to the problems which it was traditionally believed could only be met by a central government commitment through the goal of full employment and through the manipulation of macro-economic policies. Personal ownership does what central government policies cannot do. It offers a solid minimum of dignity and status for all – which 'they' cannot take away or confer at bureaucratic will. It provides the basic conditions in which 'work' and 'occupation' no longer have of necessity to be of the full-time, full-life kind in order to make ends meet. The opportunities for people to spread their mix of work activities, to perform work which they enjoy and which is socially useful, even if not highly rewarded, are vastly increased. Pursued to the full, the social aims of wider ownership becomes in fact the weapon by which the debilitating concept of the labour scrapheap can finally be razed.

The key question and challenge for the policy makers (and it is an immediate one here and now in the mid eighties in Britain) is this: how are these crucial connections to be made? What moves people to see that their values and ideals, both for themselves, their families and the communities in which they live, are more likely to be realised through widespread personal ownership in society than through traditional ideas of centralised social ownership?

Ferdinand Mount, a former policy adviser to Margaret Thatcher and a former head of her policy unit at No. 10 Downing Street, has written tellingly on this issue and in a way that those who seek to shape Conservative thinking about the future should have taken up much more vigorously.[1] He argues that widespread property ownership is inseparable from a widespread sense of obligation. 'Private property' he contends, 'is a concept which embraces and nourishes the idea of service to others. Personal ownership is not the same as self-interest. It contains an altruistic element which generalised state ownership lack, and which is indeed drained away by state domination in the welfare and 'caring' services.[2] There are echoes here once again of Alexis de Tocqueville's powerful concept of 'self interest rightly understood' – the quality he discerned in the vigorous young American society of the 1830s. What de Tocqueville was speaking about then, and what Ferdinand Mount seems to be writing about now, is a kind of tempered self-interest which, far from being rooted in greed and selfishness actually combats 'damn-the-next-man' individualism and which seems very clearly to be measured not only by a personal but by a social standard. De Tocqueville correctly identified, even in the raw American society at which he was looking, a perfectly natural and fundamental impulse towards co-operation in human affairs. He saw this as no more satisfied by an exclusive insistence on individual rights than by an insistence on strict equality and collectivised state power. Both pointed in false directions.

This instinct to co-operate, in the family, the locality or the wider community, is the one which central state power kills

1. Ferdinand Mount 'Property and Poverty' 1984 Autumn Address to the Centre for Policy Studies.
2. Ibid.

and dispersed power and ownership nourishes. It is least likely
to develop where people and policy-makers think in terms of
wages-versus-capital, where they are pre-occupied with pay
rates and with the security, and insecurity, of reliance on paid
work to maintain living standards. It is least likely to flourish
where people believe that the week's wage stands between
them and personal catastrophe.

It was de Tocqueville's observation, too, that the European
feudal and despotic traditions provided the worst possible
conditions for the emergence of his more tempered and moder-
ated sort of self interest. In Europe, extreme paternalism
guaranteed its own reaction. It ensured that the pendulum
swung either towards rampant anarchic individualism, elevated
to absurd heights of principle, or to a new brand of state
despotism. He did not add, although he might well have done,
that if we were not careful, we might in Europe end up with
both – both the attitude that responsibility for each other's
welfare and for our neighbours could all be shuffled on to an
enormous state, and the belief that unrestrained individualism
should be left to dominate the private sector field.

The Wrong Middle Way

Yet something very like that has certainly occurred – a sort of
market socialism which embodies the worst aspects of the two
philosophies, a large state and a selfish private sector. Here we
have the intellectual makings of the 'middle way' which has so
confused and befuddled British political thought. Naturally,
goes this 'middle way' line of thought, we are against Orwellian
state control. But we are also against a completely individualistic
society. It follows that the right 'half-and-half' is to have a
strong intervening welfare state, leaving people with a clearly
delineated area in which they can 'do their own thing'.
Responsibility is nationalised whilst the economy is privatised.
Thus emerges the muddled basis of contemporary ideas for a
return to the mixed socialist and capitalist economy broadly
favoured by the moderate left, the so-called centre political
parties in Britain and some members of the Conservative party
as well.

The deep error in this kind of thinking is that it seeks to draw
the middle line along the wrong axis. By contrast, the 'middle
way' to which de Tocqueville points is the one which leads each

individual in society to recognise and accept both his or her social and individual responsibilities, not only rights but also duties and obligations. Social obligations are fostered in each one of us, not divided out and allocated to quite separate sections of society. The mistake of the 'middle' way proponents of the mixed economic order has been again and again to assume that the collective and co-operative aspects of life have to be largely the responsibility of the central state, something to be handled by 'them'. This is not at all what Dr. Ludwig Erhard meant by the social market economy in the 1950s although it appears to be what Dr. David Owen means today by the social market economy. Erhard meant that the state should have a very subdued role and pursue policies based on sound conservative finance, while individuals should and would act in a wider interest than their own, if only they were left the resources to do so, and not taxed into inertia.[1] Dr. Owen seems to see things differently. In his thinking the state and the large collectivist institutions continue to be assigned a significant role, one in which government and industry form some kind of partnership and in which the individual is left to operate in a limited market sector.[2]

One can see how someone who has previously been committed to unreconstructed socialist ideas would begin to make concessions and move towards market economics along these lines. But it is the kind of thinking which leads straight into a siding. A middle way between collectivism and individualism has to be one which gives people the time and opportunity to act as they would naturally wish to do, both to reduce their dependence and enlarge their personal economic freedom. The real aim of a mixed economy should be to provide the conditions in which as many people as possible have the time and the resources to work outside their paid jobs in the services of others, to fulfil their recognised social obligations. The more that these conditions can be achieved, and of course personal ownership of capital is a very powerful agent in bringing this situation about, the more truly will substance and meaning be given to the idea of the social market economy which Erhard had right but Owen has a bit wrong. Are these sorts of mixed motivations are idealist fantasy? Will narrow self interest will

1. Dr. Ludwig Erhard, *Prosperity Through Competition*, Thames & Hudson 1958.
2. Dr. David Owen *A Future that Will Work* p. 15 Penguin 1984.

always prevail, as taught by Adam Smith?[1] Anyone who believes it should study just how much work people on extremely modest incomes do in fact undertake for nominal pay or on a voluntary basis already. This confirms the immense power of the human instinct to act socially, as opposed to collectively, in even the most hostile circumstances. People want to be free to fulfil their obligations to each other, their families, neighbourhood, and communities, if only they were allowed to keep the resources to do so. It is these resources which the high tax enthusiasts of the political Centre (so-called) and the Left want to take away.

On from Market Economics
The time and resources needed to make these social conditions a reality must come primarily from ownership, and from the culture which grows up in conditions in which personal and family ownership of homes and shares are accepted as the normal arrangement. These are not conditions which emerge automatically from market economics. Nor did they do so in early America. Governments intervened decisively, not to take away and centralise social responsibilities, not to do deals with the big interests, but to ensure that capital really was spread widely. The American government did this by the expedient of allocating small parcels of land and discouraging (admittedly not entirely effectively) the accumulation of these into large holdings.

Today's pure market economists who reject all intervention in favour of the invisible hand have therefore fundamentally misunderstood the nature of a healthy capitalist society. If the market economy is to deliver more effectively than socialism, it is essential that it should be associated with policies to promote wider capital ownership and share ownership, and the maximum dispersal of monopoly power. There has to be some reassurance, which a general disposition in favour of market economies cannot alone provide, however vigorously promoted by political leaders, that modern democratic capitalism can come to grips directly with the chief anxieties of our time – namely

1. 'It is not from the benevolence of the butcher, the brewer or the baker, that we expect our dinner, but from their regard for their own interest. We address ourselves not to their humanity, but to their self-love . . .' *The Wealth of Nations*, page 21 (Cadell & Davies, Longman et al. 1812).

poverty, unemployment and social deprivation, and to do so much more efficiently than either out-of-date state socialism or the half-and-half varieties so much in fashion in Britain's centre parties.

There is a further factor which must now be taken into account. The de Tocqueville insights from long ago have been given a fresh relevance by the arrival of the information age and the era of the microcomputer. The instinct for people to combine and co-operate on an everyday human scale, rather than turn to big government for protection, has now been given an enormously powerful reinforcement through modern technology. Industry can now operate competitively on a much smaller scale. Micro-computing power is proving to be a liberating, fragmenting, aggregate-dissolving force. It de-massifies. It makes widespread capital ownership both more possible and more appropriate. That in turn paves the way for the reinforcement of the social values and attitudes which give less weight to central state action and more emphasis and opportunities to individuals' and groups' responsibility and enterprise. Thus we have here a remarkable coincidence of forces and trends which cry out for recognition and encouragement.

We see a healthy instinct to co-operate and associate, existing alongside an equally healthy instinct towards individual expression, and determination to preserve and enlarge personal freedoms. We see a society which is clearly rejecting centralising socialist ideas – ideas which seek to exploit and distort the cooperative side of human nature – but is also plainly uneasy about placing too much faith in doctrines resting solely on the elevation of individual rights and interests. Instead, people seem to be groping for a new combination of self-reliance and cooperation which fits neither of the established philosophies. Reinforcing all this we are now in an age in which full-time paid work is no longer available to all, in which industry and commerce no longer require large numbers of unskilled people full-time, and in which it is anyway becoming more convenient for many workers, especially women, to work in their own time, often part-time, and in a more personalised way. And now, marching in alongside all these already highly significant trends we have modern micro-technology working powerfully in the same direction, weakening the case for centralism, dispersing economic power and shifting the balance of rewards sharply away from full-time labouring activity and in favour of capital equipment and products with a major intellectual content.

The common strand which threads these different scenes together is dispersed and broadened personal ownership of capital resources. Of course, it would be naive to depict a drive towards the share economy and the great spread of capital ownership as the single answer to the social problems which modern society contains. In politics there is always a regrettable tendency to demand much too much of new ideas, and then when they are found wanting to discard them. Keynesian proposals for tackling unemployment and demand deficiency were hailed as saving capitalism. But after a while they could not cope with post-war demand excess and inflation. Monetarism cannot cope with structural and technological unemployment and under-employment, although it has belatedly played a part in creating a world disinflationary climate.

Is the Valley Really Dying?
In the same way, a far stronger commitment to widened personal ownership as a major social goal, and as the inspiration behind social and industrial policy, cannot possibly 'solve' all the problems of, for example, an ex-mining community with 22% unemployment and a scattering of new factories in a nearby industrial estate. What on earth is the relevance, it will be asked, of wide individual ownership to the dereliction and despair of that sort of sadly typical scene? Yet it would be a serious mistake to dismiss the entire drive for personal ownership as having nothing important to do in such areas of our country.

Let us take a typical valley townlet, half its small shops closed, the pit due to close soon, the steel-processing plant long since shut. The boarded-up shops will only open up again, life will only grow busy and prosperous again, if people with capital and ideas are prepared to invest in the locality, which in turn will be because 'there's money about'. The factories which already employ a few people on the industrial estate can make a first beginning by installing profit-sharing schemes, maybe graduating to share option and then share distribution schemes. In the schools, the basic mechanics of enterprise as the source of employment can be taught, drawing on local examples. Home ownership can be further encouraged and local council estates privatised and modernised. Ironically it is probably the high incidence of home ownership in mining communities which has given them such cohesion and resilience – as shown in the misguided 1984–85 miners' strike.

So it is that this spirit – the spirit of belonging, of having a stake as well as deep roots, of being an integral part of society, of refusing to be left outside it – turns out to be not at all irrelevant. On the contrary it is the central ingredient of revival. It is precisely the attitude which, properly nourished, can lift depressed and 'dead' communities back to pride and prosperity. What a disappointment it was to see so little recognition of this fundamental point, this living spark of hope and creativity, in that soulless Church of England Report 'Faith in the City' which appeared towards the end of 1985. What the clerics and their associates seemed unable to grasp is how deeply destructive the 'we-they', wages-versus-capital view of the social order really is. The truly creative motivation that must somehow be restarted in the inner urban areas comes from the entirely opposite outlook. In the former case the assumption is that wage employment has got to come from somewhere, from someone from outside, from 'them' – and when it comes it always seems inadequate, wrongly given, temporary and ineffective. The latter, the ownership approach goes the other way. It gives every family the seed of an idea that they can be part of the recovery process and of the growth of their community, *from within*, that they can share as stake-holders rather than waiting to have the decisions of others, often seemingly taken on another planet, imposed upon them.

There is no need to be too restrictive about the initial form which 'capital' takes. All forms of experimentation should be welcomed and encouraged – a sort of 'capitalist Darwinism'. One could be talking about shares in the local firm, or redundancy money, or shares distributed by central government on a national basis as part of a sustained and deliberate policy for widening ownership and placing income producing assets in the hands of the vast majority of the people.[1] Or one could be talking about the straightforward spread to more employers and firms of the practice of paying lump sum bonuses twice yearly, as well as basic wages – an almost universal practice, incidentally, in Japan. Nor is it of decisive importance whether local

1. This is the approach which Samuel Brittan calls 'citizen ownership'. Something like it has been tried in British Columbia, where shares in public utilities and enterprises have been distributed to all adults.

capital is invested in long-term assets, or whether it is spent on home improvement and the upgrading of existing physical assets. The essential point is that these are resources which visibly and tangibly belong to people. Capital begins to share the stage with wages. Ownership and the handling and the investment of savings become not 'for the likes of others' but for the likes of every family in the community.

It can of course be argued that the injection of funds into the community by central government policy through the capital route is really no different from upping social security payments to low income families who have been left high and dry by structural change – by the pit closing or the steel mill contracting. But there is every diffeence in the world between income coming regularly from the state through some bureaucratic system, at a rate determined by remote political decision, and income flowing from one's own lawfully owned personal property. 'A source of income', Samuel Brittan reminds us, 'unconnected with either work or state handouts has always been a source of security and independence'. It is those two qualities – security and independence – which are the vital ingredients for enterprise and recovery in any village, any town, any valley or any region. That is why the social goal of much wider personal ownership, far from being marginal to the horrific problems of the depressed mining communities, or of derelict inner city areas, is a completely central consideration, the 'micro' key to recovery, improvement and regeneration, which decades of macro-economic strategy has not been able to provide.

Concentric Circles of Capitalism
In *Freedom and Capital*,[1] I sought to depict the spread of ownership in a modern society as moving outward in concentric circles. At the inner core, I suggested, we should place the 3 million or so people who already own shares directly in companies, who are already comfortable and familiar with the habits of equity ownership and of relying on a second income or resource to be called upon from outside their main paid work. In short, for families in this category their status and self-confidence already rests on what they own as well as what they

1. Blackwell 1981.

earn. At the outer rim of the ownership circle, I placed those families which are just beginning to be accustomed to the idea of being owners, of 'saving up a little bit', as Iain Macleod put it in his famous 1965 speech to the Conservative Party Conference, where he dwelt prophetically on the theme of the nationwide capital-owning democracy. In between lie the groups of families who have begun to think of owning as well as earning, begun to put money into unit trusts, have received a few employee shares from the firm, maybe bought a new Telecom shares or (and this is for the future) received some national share of asset under a citizen ownership scheme, and have decided to buy their council house instead of paying endless rent.

There is no reason at all why all these outer 'circles' should not be steadily moving towards the solid central ground of ownership as a firm, secure source of a second income and support of existing living standards. There is no reason why society should not be far more comfortable, secure and sensitive if people rely less on full time wages and more on capital resources. The policy makers' aim should be to close these rings ever more tightly together and to encourage those at the outside to move step by step into the circles of the property-owning democracy of which they can all be a part.

Of course for those who have no job at all at present and no skills or understanding of how to create a job for themselves or how to be satisfyingly occupied, the prospect of actually owning resources may seem a long way off, much further than the more immediate goal of earning a wage. Yet it could well be that the miserable and baffling phenomenon of high unemployment constitutes not a rejection of the ideal of a property-owning democracy but a direct challenge which it is more capable of meeting than other great philosophies. Welfare collectivism and income redistribution have been able neither to perpetuate the fully employment pattern of the post-war world, nor to destigmatise, nor even explain, involuntary unemployment. Nor have these broad approaches apparently sufficed to raise living standards for the mass of people sufficiently above the minimum levels of benefit and status which are generally regarded today as consistent with a civilised standard of living. What other conclusion can one draw from the fact that a third of all households are still drawing housing benefits and four million people are on supplementary benefit?

The measures now required to replace this 'knot' of traditional attitudes, to mount a genuine challenge, and not just a rhetorical one, to centralised monopoly and economic power, are not just marginal. They constitute, if properly assembled and coherently put forward, a policy for capitalism of the utmost boldness. They involve an egalitarian zeal which will seem foreign to many, although not all, Conservatives, and an active and forward government policy to promote capital distribution of the kind which may well leave conventional market economists uneasy.

The New Mood

A decade ago, the wise men and commentators spoke of the ungovernability of British society. Trade union power, they said, was unbeatable. Consumer demands were insatiable and the pressures on central government to deliver the results by magic were unsustainable. Few people accepted that wider personal ownership had any part to play in resolving the issues.

Today the 'impossible' union pressures have subsided to a far greater extent than many people hoped or expected. Trade union rank and file members are no longer willing to support militant politicised unionism blindly. Local interests are taking precedence over national class war strategies and 'profits' is no longer a dirty word. Can all this be, as the Left claim, because of the widespread fear of unemployment? To hold such a belief may comfort some and obviate the tiresome need for further political thought. But, it also blinds its adherents to the much larger forces at work in our society. Millions of people are now beginning to see themselves as potential proprietors of the economy and society, as stakeholders, rather than as cornered wage slaves, trapped completely in a subordinate employee status, whose only option is to fight the wage struggle and extract the maximum immediate gain from the boss class and from authority.

It is from an acute realisation of this new mood that the policies needed for today and tomorrow are going to come. It is from an understanding that the social and economic landscape is not only about to change but has, to a considerable extent changed already, that the urgent energy must come to tear down the intellectual road blocks which remain and open the highway which will take us out into a different landscape.

PART VI

Towards a less general theory

'The collectivists have the zest for progress, the sympathy for the poor, the burning sense of wrong, the impulse for great deeds, which have been lacking in latter-day liberalism. But their science is founded on a profound misunderstanding and their actions, therefore are deeply destructive and reactionary. So men's hearts are torn, their minds divided, they are offered impossible choices.'

Walter Lippman

CHAPTER 16

Economic Policy Now

It is now fashionable to look back on the late fifties and early sixties in Britain as a sort of golden era. Indeed, critics of the British Government's monetarist stance after 1979 have indignantly accused the monetarists of re-writing the history of Conservative Government from 1951 to 1964 in a distorting light.[1] But it has to be remembered that the policies at the time seemed dismal. The approaches to tax reform, welfare reform and labour market reform were thoroughly feeble and there was generally little faith in making markets work at the micro-level. The Conservative Bow Group, for example, was considered very avant-garde, even dangerous in those days for its enthusiasm for market economies and its interest in the social market economy ideas of the German Finance Minister and later Chancellor, Ludwig Erhard.[2]

Above all, the 1950s were a quite disastrous period for personal savings in Britain and for all those groups and classes in British society who believed in the virtues of thrift and the bourgeois values. They felt themselves, correctly, to be bypassed by the lofty preoccupations of central government with the bigger battalions of the national scene, with the broad economic and financial aggregates and with trying to make macro-economics work. The 1950s were also a very bad period for investment in new plant, equipment and infrastructure. With the habits of the war economy only slowly wearing off, too many investment decisions tended to be large, centralised and unprofitable.

For misguided reasons, largely associated with fears from pre-war days about volatile and inefficient markets leading to mass unemployment and concentrated private wealth, the Conservative Governments of those days, despite a desire 'to set the

1. See Sir Ian Gilmour, *Britain Can Work*, page 96.
2. See *Prosperity Through Competition*, Ludwig Erhard, Thames & Hudson 1958.

people free', also set much store by central intervention and influence. They believed in trying to control the aggregates and they believed that the trade union movement embraced and spoke for a comprehensive working class. In consequence, they found themselves driven into supporting large groups and interests in society and tendencies which did not mix well with small government thinking or with the kind of traditional small-scale 'people's' Conservatism which many of their followers had once supported.

Some of the rhetoric remained traditional. 'The present weight of direct taxation' said R. A. Butler 'acts as a very positive discouragement to extra effort'. This was so he announced, particularly for the lower and middle income groups.[1] But the basic attitudes were Keynesian, as Butler also admitted, and took the Government into the heart of the wrestling match with elusive and disobedient national aggregates. 'To be perfectly fair' he observed in a moment of marvellous candour somewhat later, 'my economic brief was pretty unintelligible.'[2]

The force of economic and social policy was not, therefore, in the direction it should have been, and was beginning to be in neighbouring economies. It was not towards the promotion of those individuals, interests and motivations which would have boosted personal savings massively and helped finance a vigorous programme of investment throughout Britain's battered cities and surrounding regions. In the language of those days, Britain needed a policy for restoring the confidence of the entrepreneurial and middle classes, for taking society away from two-class attitudes and from the futile general debate about the relative shares of capital and labour. That would have been the true 'middle way' which the Conservative party was well equipped to follow. But it was not, alas, what many Conservatives thought of as the middle way.

Instead, they remained convinced of the need for a policy which accepted trade union power as a fact of national life, and which entrenched the broad attitudes towards wages and profits which union leaders found politically useful and comfortable. By refusing to change the emphasis of social and taxation policy very radically, or to consider measures which would have eroded the concentrations of wealth and privilege

1. R. A. Butler, Chancellor of the Exchequer, in his 1952 Budget Speech.
2. R. A. Butler *The Art of the Possible*, page 165. Hamish Hamilton, 1971.

in society, including the state sector, and which would have distributed capital far more widely, the Conservative leaders of that era perpetuated conditions which allowed the Marxian myth of struggle between wages and capital full play, with catastrophic effects on national performance.

The consequences of the attempt to implement Mr Butler's 'unintelligible' brief were predictable. Governments found themselves increasingly trapped between confident and militant leaders of organised labour, who were deeply hostile to capital and to the smaller end of private enterprise, and a weak national performance reflected in constant pressures on a still fixed exchange rate, guarded by exchange controls. Policy bounced between these two forces in a series of stop-go episodes which further weakened investment incentives and further demoralised the very people whom central government should have been bending all its energies to encourage, and who should have been developing into a dominant ownership class. None of this happened.

It is no surprise that Keynesians in all political parties in Britain look back on this period somewhat selectively. Employment was high, real incomes were rising (although more slowly than elsewhere) and the money was being spent rather than saved. The central Government seemed to have found the secret of operating the Keynesian levers. That personal savings were low and personal interest in the use to which savings were put almost non-existent, did not matter. The state could step and and do the job. What is more curious is that, as macro-economic strategies have faltered, as unemployment has risen and stagflation taken hold, the arguments in favour of these central strategies should have persisted in both socialist and non-socialist circles, that micro-economic alternatives should have been so neglected and in particular that the potential benefits of much wider capital ownership should have been so neglected. It is as though there has been a tacit intellectual alliance between all three parts of the political spectrum. On the Left there is the wish to see the ownership question ignored, since it plainly undermines collectivist authority and class analysis. On the traditional Right there has been a willingness to accept the same class analysis for difference motives and to distrust ideas of wider capital distribution as being a threat to established power. The usual language of this school is that 'the workers are not ready for personal capital ownership'. Across the centre have reigned the attitudes of the macro-economists whose concern has to be with incomes, pay and wages and whose ideas are threatened by a switch of emphasis from income distribution to capital distribution.

This triple alliance has been enough to freeze both the economic debate and the debate on social reform. The basic monetarist insight – that economic performance depended upon micro-economic reforms rather than attempts to alter aggregate demand – ought to have broken the deadlock but it did not do so. Why not? Because the monetarists who dominated policy making in the early eighties in Britain made the same mistakes as their predecessors. They became bogged down in the pursuit of 'macro' targets, set with unrealistic precision, and they continued to think and speak about earnings and pay settlements in the same centralist terms. These 'technical' monetarists failed to grasp the central successor idea to Keynes, towards which a more balanced monetarism should have led them. They failed, or did not have the confidence, to see that a policy of central commitment to widespread capital ownership and to high personal savings could now deliver society's goals in a way which central strategies could not. They failed to see that if dignity, status and more satisfying work for all were the social aims, it was 'micro' and not 'macro' policies which would now secure them – policies aimed at the roots of the old, old problem, the inflexibility of the labour market.

The common strand through all these ideas has been the desire from the centre to exert some sort of control on the upward movement of wages and salaries while the big scale remedies work their magic. Incomes policy has become the 'other half' of national macro-economics. 'Some kind of incomes policy' has become the inseparable remedy from the rest of the Keynesian package. This is understandable. Once it had become clear in the post-war climate that the Keynesian 'by-pass' of labour market problems also by-passed the question of what to do about pay leapfrogging and soaring labour costs, the spotlight was bound to switch to pay and how it could be centrally controlled. At first the idea was to have direct wage and price controls as in wartime. However, as the difficulties and obvious unfairness of comprehensive central controls multiplied, the fashion switched to voluntary controls – which also failed to work except in the very early stages – and most recently to a class of incomes policy which is supposed to work through tax incentives. The idea is to administer from the centre a range of tax penalties on wage settlements (if the centre has recorded them correctly) which seem to be above the norm.

Schemes of this kind are favoured in Britain by the centre parties and some Conservatives. They have never been success-fully implemented. Even if central government knew in practice what wages were being paid throughout the economy, schemes like this, requiring colossal central omniscience, would be unlikely starters. In the conditions we have been examining in earlier chapters of this book they would be fantasy. Not only is the information about pay which reaches the centre becoming increasingly blurred and unreliable but, as Nicholas Kaldor recognised long ago with his proposals for a switch of taxation from income to expenditure, recorded incomes are an extremely poor measure of economic circumstance, so that controlling them is bound to be grotesquely unfair. When one adds in the realisation that, with the emergence of new work patterns, probably the majority of those working are not covered by explicit pay settlements negotiated between employers and employee representatives, the partial and quite impractical nature of this kind of thinking becomes crystal clear.

None of this has deterred leading economists from continuing to urge on policy-makers some kind of central pay control. Nor has it stopped Ministers making speeches deploring the level of wage settlements, the alleged rate of increase in average earnings, and the deplorable refusal of the labour market to settle down and work. This is because the Government remains pinned to the unattainable objective of a return to the classic form of full-employment and believes that high pay settlements will lead, if not to inflation, (although some officials still even use that language) then to more unemployment. What is not perceived fully yet is that a far greater emphasis on capital rewards as opposed to pure wages helps resolve this baffling process and that the work landscape has anyway altered radically. Quite aside from the needs of modern industry, a world in which fewer, more highly paid, people have full-time employment, while increasing numbers work for themselves, can certainly be a fairer and more compassionate one, as was argued in Part IV of this book.

CHAPTER 17

The Hope of '79

The Great Hope of 1979 in Britain was this; that the party and Government policy-makers who had been given power would recognise this new newly-emerging and wholly different landscape, would accept it rather than obstruct it and reshape both policies and its style accordingly. The whole emphasis on crude macro-economic theory and centre lever-pulling would be reversed. The hope was that the enormous bluff of the cardboard army of the trade union movement would be called. The unions had a job to do but they did not need to be solemnly consulted before every act of public policy, nor placated by a stream of measures to their supposed liking. The make-believe world of aggregatists and centralists, would be dismantled and measures brought forward in the micro-economy which would enable the new shoots in the forest to grow, the new deregulated market economy, the world of independent business, new ideas, self-employment and radically altered work patterns, to emerge and develop vigorously.

As we have seen, some of this happened but a great deal of it did not. In particular, while the new rhetoric spoke of less government and a humbler and more limited role for the central administration, the new practice clung as hard as ever to a belief in financial aggregates which had to be, could only be, adjusted and manipulated from the centre. Almost overnight we found ourselves transported back to the same over-emphasis and over-reliance on aggregate concepts – this time, monetarist ones – that had so rightly attracted the ridicule of Nicholas Kaldor and others two decades before. The old tyrants of demand management and incomes policy had been toppled, but the new tyrants of the monetary aggregates and of the Public Sector Borrowing Requirement had been enthroned in their place.

Thus the generalists remained very much in charge, both in the Cabinet and in Whitehall. Those of us who believed that macro-economics was dead, or at least dying, and that the nature of the business cycle had changed would have to wait a little longer. Where the new dirigism of 1979 sprang from one cannot be sure. In Opposition the Conservatives had rightly been careful about exaggerating the benefits and miracles which would flow from successful control of the money supply. The economic statement of 1977, The Right Approach to the Economy, very carefully avoided making too many claims in this area and putting too much weight on controlling the monetary aggregates above all else.[1] These things we recognised as important but uncertain and vague, not an area in which one staked all the political chips on numbers and concepts which might not turn out the way they looked, or might prove in the British context to be maddeningly unreliable and uncontrollable.

Paradoxically the circumspect Conservative approach in opposition was in some respects more radical than the one adopted by the new Treasury team. There was strong sympathy for the idea that monetary policy, although not the be-all and end-all, was too important and complex to be left in the centre of the political arena, and that we could do worse than follow the German example of placing monetary judgments in more independent hands. In other words, if the Bank of England could be given the independence from the politicians of, for example, the German Bundesbank the management of monetary policy could be taken out of the front line, over-selling of monetarism avoided, and government policy generally presented in a less abstract and dessicated form.

But by the time the Cabinet got down to these things in May 1979 this kind of caution and prudence was gone. The PSBR was enthroned, with the Medium-Term Financial Strategy already brewing. Unyielding formulae, automatic pilots, tram-line strategies were 'in'. A finger in the wind, a weather eye to changing conditions and a nose for a coming storm were 'out', as some of us discovered when we tried to raise these matters calmly in discussion. Especially unwelcome was any suggestion that the soaring price of crude oil (which was to triple in the twelve months after May 1979) had changed the ground under our feet and made the central imposition of a rigid harness of monetary aggregates even less appropriate. On the contrary, came the answer, if the oil price explosion was changing all the

---

1. *The Right Approach to the Economy*, published by Conservative Central Office. This had five authors, Geoffrey Howe, Jim Prior, Keith Joseph, Angus Maude and myself.

parameters, it was all the more important for Government to stick to the same tracks.

Although the 1979 stance was therefore wrongly balanced from the start it is possible to have some sympathy with the viewpoints which underlay it. The dragons to be slain – inflation and excessive union power – were powerfully and centrally entrenched. It was always going to need crude weapons crudely used to root them out. Some over-reaction against the high nonsenses of public policy in the seventies was understandable, and perhaps inevitable. Yet what was indubitably vexing was to see these early impulses lead on not to a complete reassessment of the role and limits of central government in macroeconomic policy but to the enthronement of another set of questionable aggregates at the centre of economic policy-making.

Almost from the outset in 1979 it became impossible to question the component elements of the Public Sector Borrowing Requirement, the ways in which it came to be defined, whether its size determined interest rates (subsequent developments showed that for the UK the connection was tenuous), whether some forms of expenditure restraint affected it more than others, whether some cuts might actually increase it, whether judgments about its appropriate size should take account of outside circumstances and so on. To aim strategically for lower public borrowing, taking account of world recession and longer term infrastructure needs, was one thing. To elevate a specific number as the annual PSBR target, and to make its achievement a priority aim of political policy, overriding other valid policy aims, seemed to me to be a recipe for taking high risks with thoroughly unreliable statistics, for much egg on many faces and for straining public credulity to breaking point. It was to put the Treasury's viewpoint first without any qualification or reflection, and thus to deter, indeed to freeze, innovative thinking in other departments. The apex of absurdity during this phase was the 1981 Budget[1] judgment which has been hailed as some sort of Stalingrad, the moment when the dark forces of ever rising public expenditure were finally and heroically turned. Yet not only was the trimming of the PSBR forecast, the focus of political concern, from £13.5 billion to £10.5 billion

---

1. See, for example, Patrick Cosgrave's interesting assessment of the 1981 Budget as 'the crucial event of the first Thatcher term'. *Thatcher: The First Term*, p. 121 (The Bodley Head).

achieved extensively by cuts in capital programmes (which would have miserable consequences two to three years later), but subsequent events confirmed that the thing was grossly overdone. It had to be defended publicly, but in truth the ten billion pound figure announced might just as well have been twelve billion. The argument was that a higher figure would raise interest rates or revive inflation or undermine financial market confidence. But no facts or subsequent events have ever been identified to support these contentions. If Britain had been a single, closed national economic entity they might have had some validity, provided that one could rely on the aggregate concepts lying behind the Borrowing Requirement itself, which one cannot. But the idea that in a wide open medium-sized economy like the British, operating amidst global pressures far greater than anything that could be mounted from within, fine-tuning adjustments in the aggregates of the kind demanded could have such mechanically decisive effects, was of course ridiculous. 1981 was no Stalingrad. It was a largely unnecessary battle, based on narrow understanding of the limits of policy-making, and delaying economic recovery. The story ended with an ironical twist. A year later the actual figure turned out to be £8.6 billion, far lower than planned. Most of the hassle had been unnecessary.

The misjudgments of this unhappy period came primarily, I believe, not from 'monetarism' or a reluctance to attempt some Keynesian reflation. They came from an exaggerated and quite outdated view of the precision with which national governments could influence the major economic and financial aggregates. In the end this precision impressed no one. It subtracted from rather than added to the general level of confidence in financial markets. In the ensuing years the economic policy-makers have had to step back and back from these numbers and targets and concede reality. The figures are vague, the influences and pressures are vast and international. The wise course is to struggle in the direction of rough budgetary balance, possibly with an overshoot to be funded which is broadly equivalent to the capital-flavoured element in the public budget, but not on any account to make this the political centrepiece.

CHAPTER 18

Monetarism: A New Modesty

'I hate people' wrote William Hazlitt, 'who have no notion of anything but generalities, and forms, and creeds, and naked propositions.'[1] We must, he argued, begin with people, with individuals, not with categories and corporations. We must suspect great aggregates and generalisations and we must equally suspect those on whose lips these general propositions hang. They are nearly always an escape from reality, which is complicated, unquantifiable, surprising and marvellously varied.

It seems to me that this attitude, which was always deeply right and from which successive generations of busy, central-ising ideologues would have greatly benefitted, is becoming more and more appropriate, indeed essential, as the starting point for policy-makers in central government today. Aggrega-tism was a dangerous infection amongst policy-makers before the fragmentation of modern market economies began to accel-erate with the onset of micro-electronics and information tech-nology. It is becoming entirely out of place in the new conditions.

This over-dependence on central government to 'solve' society's economic problems does seem to be uniquely strong in Britain as compared with the other advanced industrial coun-tries. It is frequently claimed that an unwavering central govern-ment commitment to a tight monetary stance as the best anti-dote to inflation is shared by all the OECD Finance Ministers and the governments behind them.[2] But this completely over-looks the point that the architects of German, French, Italian or Japanese social reform have followed a significantly different

1. 'Essay on Reason and Imagination.'
2. See, for example, Nigel Lawson's statement to Lancashire businessmen of 23rd June 1985 which referred to 'the remarkable international consensus which has emerged about the nature of the problems faced by Britain and many other developed countries, and their solution'.

path from their British counterparts and that their monetary and budgetary policies have only formed one aspect of their overall strategy.

Of course the British 'technical' monetarists have argued vigorously that their policies are entirely different from anything that has gone before. First they point out that there is a different approach to wages. Wage militancy now works out in unemployment rather than inflation. This does not seem to prevent Government Ministers making speeches pleading for wage restraint of a kind which sounds depressingly similar to those made by Selwyn Lloyd twenty-five years ago. But there can be no doubt that these pleas also contain a new element – namely the argument that not only will large wage increase settlements destroy jobs but that wages must be flexible downwards if labour markets are to be cleared and people priced into work. We have seen in an earlier chapter that this is a message which if presented baldly and in the wrong context, is received by the electorate with very little enthusiasm indeed.

Second, until very recently the simpler-minded monetarists have stuck to the theory that external exchange rate movements do not matter very much. It is the domestic monetary situation which matters. Either the currency markets will settle down of their own accord. Or, if they continue to oscillate wildly there is nothing very much that can be done about it. At least, goes the argument, there will be no sterling crises as in the old days, which violent changes in the domestic fiscal stance and in interest rates whenever a currency storm occurs.

The weakness in this stance lies, as it lay all along, not so much in its internal logic as in its failure to take account, first of the very strong, indeed probably dominant, external influences on the open British economy and, second, of the extremely crude and unscientific nature of monetary control. The inflation rate has been falling right across the world for several years. It has fallen in Germany and Japan – much further and faster than in Britain. It has fallen in Socialist France.[1] It has fallen in Italy, where there has been no policy of any kind to restrain wages – although at least the automatic linking of wages to prices has been abandoned. And it has fallen substantially in the United States and continues to fall. What we are seeing are the consequences of a world disinflationary climate

---

1. Now under a mixed Left/Right regime.

with weak oil and commodity prices and with an underlying pattern of consumer demand which is changing fast and reducing quite dramatically the world hunger for raw materials. Almost every raw material, including foodstuffs, is in substantial surplus. It is not just the link between oil and economic growth which has been broken. Raw material producers across the world are finding the markets flat for their products even in conditions of steady economic growth in the industrialised world.

Of course it remains possible for individual national governments to create inflation within their own national boundaries by wildly expansionary and monetarily irresponsible policies. If the British in the first years of the 1980s had run their annual borrowing requirements at £15 billion or £20 billion a year, rather than £10 billion and then lower figures beyond that, this would certainly have created inflation, even in a world disinflationary climate, or might have prevented the inflation rate falling. But provided that borrowing was kept within reasonable limits and properly financed by the sale of gilt edged stock, all the evidence suggests that inflation was anyway due to come down steadily over the first half of the decade. Keeping within precise monetary brackets, or attempting to do so, and driving the public sector borrowing requirement progressively downwards as a percentage of GDP, probably made very little difference indeed to the overall downward inflationary trend.

Naturally, the policy-makers who have been advocating very tight and very precise monetary targets have loudly claimed otherwise and have insisted they are truly the ones with their hands on the levers. 'We have reduced inflation' is anyway an irresistible claim for a government to make. When inflation rises, Ministers are invariably blamed so why should they not take a little credit when the inflation rate falls. For the high church monetarists in London it has been especially necessary to establish that all credit is theirs for what is in fact a world wide trend because they have been the ones who have persistently rejected all arguments for a more moderate monetarist line, have allowed exchange rates to rise in the early eighties to astronomical heights and have put spending programmes through the wringer, all in the cause of tight and precise monetary control. It would therefore be an impossible embarrassment if the suggestion gained credence that the fall in inflation arose primarily from international causes.

But even if – despite the overwhelming evidence – tight domestic monetary policy really were the *main* downward influence on inflation in the United Kingdom, has the government really got the power to control the monetary aggregates? Does it even know what those aggregates are and how they are going to behave? Almost certainly not, or to anything like the precise degree claimed by the monetary 'engineers' of the early 1980s. Not only is there the basic problem about the velocity with which money circulates, and the tendency for different types of 'money' to proliferate. It has gradually dawned that the various indicators of money supply being used are totally unreliable. So-called 'broad money', it is now recognised, has little causal link with inflation. Its main driving force is bank lending which is motivated by deeper forces in an expanding economy than those which can be touched by pulling the monetary levers. With the arrival of high technology in banking all kinds of new ways have been found for expanding credit which policy cannot touch. Even the narrower definitions of 'money', which the layman would more readily recognise, the actual 'money' used in transactions, have begun to blur confusingly, driving some experts to the view that the safest course is simply to try and target the money value (nominal value) of the Gross Domestic Product each year and reinforce this endeavour by having much more explicit exchange rate policies as well.

In practice both fiscal and monetary policy were tighter during most of the Macmillan years than they have been during the eighties. Despite a great deal of noise and theory over public expenditure and the borrowing requirement, the actual borrowing needs of government have been running in the first half of the present decade at about the same modest level as they were pitched in the fifties, having been pushed upwards in the very early eighties by extra demands from unemployment pay and lower-than-expected revenues due to lower economic activity. For the most part the PSBR has wended its own way, making fairly good nonsense year after year of the targets proclaimed in advance by the Treasury and the Chancellor. In all probability the current expenditure budget of the central government has been just about in balance in recent years, with borrowing concerning most, but not all, capital spending. (One must, however, be careful about describing all so-called government capital spending as 'investment' – and therefore financeable by borrowing – as some would like to do. From the point of view of the lender, government spending is government spending, however officialdom describes it.)

None of this should be taken to mean that the size of government borrowing does not matter, as the severe anti-monetarists assert, or that the monetary aggregates do not matter at all in so far as they can be measured. But it suggests that a new modesty is needed in handling monetary policy. It offers a strong warning about the severe limits of macro-economic policy making – a warning which of course applied just as much to the Keynesian demand managers as to the monetarists struggling with their targets. The answer to the vagaries and inadequacies of one form of macro-economic policy is not another macro-economic nostrum. It is to recognise that the struggle for better economic performance has to be fought on the micro-economic front and that the general world of aggregates and central control is becoming a less and less suitable place from which to influence society's economic stability and development.

The saga of the PSBR merely confirms that monetary theory, although it contains important insights and a strong dose of commonsense, rests on uncertain ground. It emphasises the extreme unwisdom of putting macro-economic policy too much at the centre of the government's strategy and general approach. To do so, to elevate complex and unreliable financial factors into a political philosophy is to ask for trouble, which is indeed what the British Conservative government found itself receiving in ample measure. This also explains why the British government, as it gradually became aware of these weaknesses in its arguments, belatedly but entirely rightly, sought to turn the debate on to the micro-economic issue and to downgrade macro-economic policy. In the autumn of 1985 officialdom finally admitted, through the mouth of the Chancellor of the Exchequer, that for an open economy like the British the monetary indicator Sterling M3 was so unreliable as to be entirely useless.[1] A further and less explicit admission was that the sterling exchange rate mattered to the policy makers rather more than pure monetarists liked to admit and that the exchange rate, as well as some of the still surviving monetary indi-

1. Nigel Lawson at the Mansion House, November 1985.

cators, would be used to reach judgments about the appropriate monetary and fiscal posture domestically.

The danger in making this switch of emphasis, aside from the embarrassment that it causes some advisers and Ministers who have previously sold absurdly over-precise monetary policies, is that it immediately allows reflationists to claim a victory. This is precisely what has now happened. The situation has been further confused by the Government's decision to accelerate the sales of state assets as part of its privatisation programme and to use the additional proceeds to finance maintained high levels of public spending, as well as some extra public spending, as well again as trying to keep some room for tax cuts. Finally, the government has at last begun to take a less rigid attitude towards precise PSBR targets themselves, being ready to contemplate the odd overshoot of a billion or so in public sector borrowing, providing the reasons are clearly stated.[1] All this has led not just the reflationists and the Government's critics but a good many suspicious City analysts to conclude that monetary policy has somehow been relaxed and that inflation may lie ahead. This is a point which the debate has now reached.

The dangers of claiming too much for monetarism, which were apparent to many politicians and laymen long before 1979, and certainly when the full and detailed rigours of the medium term financial strategy were presented to a bemused Cabinet after the Conservative victory are now clearly becoming apparent to the technical monetarists as well. The Conservative government, like its predecessors, is now back in the position of pleading for wage restraint, fearing that it may have to raise interest rates sharply if sterling weakens and hoping that international forces will keep inflation down. However, these forces could go too far, too fast. Obviously if they took the world crude oil price not just to $15 but to the $10 level (which is not impossible) this would yet again postpone the opportunity for the major tax cuts that the Conservative Chancellor has been promising a highly expectant army of Conservative supporters.

---

1. *E.g.* in the case of public expenditure arising from the coalminers' strike, 1984. Some commentators have argued that the same upward 'slide' could be prudently allowed to compensate for lost oil revenues as well.

CHAPTER 19

The New Setting

Thus successive post-war British Government have had their dalliance with macro-economics and each in turn have found themselves coming up against a stubborn reality. This reality is that the British economy, which has become increasingly open and is floating in a sea of world pressures, cannot be precisely controlled or influenced by national government policy in London. Internationally, the world economy is far more closely integrated, while internally the aggregates upon which government relied to control the economy have crumbled. The hope after 1979 was that the policy-makers would not make the same mistakes as their predecessors. The hope was that macro-economics would be put as far as possible aside – indeed outside politics altogether, if that could be achieved – and that the concentration from the start would be on the micro-economic 'supply side'.

Had this approach been followed, either under Macmillan or during the first years of Mrs. Thatcher's administration, it is hard to resist the thoughts that the whole Parliamentary and political battle might have looked very different. The thirteen years of Conservative rule to 1964 might have been extended to twenty-five or the present Conservative period might have begun to look much more like the opening period of a long and sustained era of confident Conservative rule which the architects of 1979 wanted it to be, and less like a risky direction less hanging-on operation which may just, with luck, lead to a third Conservative term if fortune favours the Tories.

It is by no means too late to change the emphasis of Conservative policy in good time to win the next election comfortably and confidently. Indeed the process of change has already begun. Admittedly, the whole picture has been obscured by the chopping and changing of official macro-economic thinking, leading bewildered City commentators to conclude that monetary prudence has been abandoned, and that the British economy is out of control. And by the standards which were set up by both Keynesian and monetarist 'aggregatists' against which 'control' was supposed to be measured, this is an understandable conclusion. But the real seriousness of this is not that it confuses the economic pundits. That could scarcely matter less. The danger is more political. It is that the Government looks as though it no longer understands how the world works, as though it is deluded by its own myths.

A new explanation and a new framework of reference are now urgently required. Both existing and new policies need to be given the proper philosophical setting. A string of measures mean nothing except argument and confusion, if people do not understand how they fit together and where they are heading. This is not just a question of presentation in the usual journalistic sense, of hapless Ministers being pushed into 'selling' government policy via weekend handouts listing the ten steps the government has taken, is taking or promises to take, to achieve this or that. The task of explaining what the government is trying to do, and how the government sees society today, how it evaluates all the different concerns and anxieties in society and how it thinks about these issues and plans to respond to them, is overwhelmingly an intellectual task.

Intellectual insights into the changing character of society, based not on vague theory but on an acute appreciation of every day events, changing practices, altering patterns of life and ordinary feelings in face of these changes, provided the foundation for the Conservative case in the 1960s and the 1970s. In consequence it was a very powerful one indeed and in the event electorally victorious. The synthesis of that time gave momentum to the Conservatives to defeat their opponents' arguments, and the energies needed to drive forward new measures and legislation in line with the new vision. It was this intellectual drive which gave birth to measures for trade union reform, for privatisation, for de-regulation, for council house sales, for initial (although so far less than needed) tax reforms, for amendment of penal capital taxes and for small business incentives, and which also made those measures acceptable to the public, far more acceptable than many journalists and politicians who were privy to the Conservatives' plans expected or predicted. Even those Conservatives who fully supported the new ideas and were fully committed to the rejection of incomes policies and the consensus thinking of the seventies,

were surprised to find how easily the door opened when
pushed and how hollow and feeble the opposition, both at
Westminster and in Fleet Street, actually proved to be.

But in one crucial era, this questioning and thrusting intellectual impetus failed. It did not extend to the high and pure
monetary doctrines which the government eagerly embraced as
soon as it took office,. The country was just not prepared for
the primacy which was given to precise national monetary
targets and to the Medium Term Financial Strategy. Nor did
people understand why something so speculative and abstract
should demand the subjugation of the whole of the rest of
Conservative policy. The MTFS was never likely to be, and is
certainly not now, an intelligible political goal worth working
for or making sacrifices for.

The Conservatives now badly need to mobilise their intellectual reserves and root their own vision in a thorough understanding of today's attitudes, outlook and conditions. Policies
make no sense unless they fit into a picture. Able public
relations men cannot be expected to step in and cobble together
some overnight theme as a substitute for these solid intellectual
foundations. Neither the dilapidated dogmas of collectivism,
nor the simplicities of liberal market economics answer the need
or offer the ideas which help people understand the world
which has emerged with such amazing speed around them and
their families.

The 'large and liberal' vision of today and tomorrow must be
one which shows the path to dignity and status for all in the
new conditions which technology has both imposed and now
permits. To found that vision on a call for a return to full-
employment, or on some discredited macro-economic formu-
lation, is to insult people's commonsense appreciation of the
way the world now works. Even if it makes Conservatives
uncomfortable, the new political vision must be realistically
international, it must also be egalitarian – although not in the
income-levelling, socialist sense. The principle with which we
should be concerned is one of 'egalitarianism rightly understood', if one may borrow from and adapt de Tocqueville's
principle of 'self interest rightly understood'. It needs to be the
widely appreciated aim that government, recognising its own
changing role in a more informed and dispersed society, is
vigorously committed to the spread of ownership (and its
associated duties) and the dismantling of monopoly concen-

tration of power, without the exceptions and qualifications which erode the whole vision and make people question whether anything is really changing at all.

The test of that commitment is to see whether the government is really prepared to put conventional macro-economic solutions, Keynesian or monetarist, more to one side, whether it is prepared to tackle the old macro-economic problems at their source. Is it prepared to turn its hand to policies which will truly and radically reform the labour market by reforming the system and custom of rewards in society? It is prepared to even up fiscal privilege as between individuals and institutions, give powerful incentives to ownership as well as to employee earnings, dismember the remaining monopolies (or allow technology to do so) and lift the barriers and restrictions which remain in the way of 'auto-dynamic' activities of all kinds? These things will be the real measure of the change of policy emphasis needed. Very bold steps and very innovative thought are required.

First, the policy makers will have to be prepared to downgrade macro-economic policy as a strategic political plank, to accept that general, central and nationally conceived strategies are no longer the best way of achieving the main economic and social goals of society.

Second, they will need to peer through and beyond the work attitudes and practices associated with full-time, full-career employment and to appreciate the narrow and declining relevance of this whole approach. They will need to recognise that the opportunities for paid work, for partly paid work and for valuable but unpaid work in a new and more disorganised but much more flexible labour market are inexhaustible.

Third, they will need to acknowledge the severe limitation which orthodox thinking about pay and work places in the way of a fully-occupied society, of general economic stability and development.

Fourth, they will need to accept fully the new responsibilities which the situation now imposes on them – namely to ensure that resources, including both capital and income, are distributed by the market economy on the widest possible basis, regardless of whether the recipients are paid employees or self-employed, full-time or part-time, men or women, beyond present definitions of retirement age or not. They will need to promote the share economy through every channel of policy as an idea, as an ideal and as a practicable, attainable reform of the labour market and of the whole economic system.

Fifth, they will need to recognise that these responsibilities mean ensuring that capital and ownership really are genuinely and enduringly spread, that people are educated and trained to live comfortably in the post-full-employment era, that there is no scrapheap in society.

A government which develops its policies and thinking on these lines will find that it is moving with the stream, instead of becoming more and more unpopular and out of connection with the pattern of events, as seemed to be the fate of the Conservative administration in the mid-1980s. It is really the idea of large-scale economic policy itself which is under challenge. The new directions and new priorities lead not towards yet another economic policy in the post-war sense, but to a series of social, educational, industrial and fiscal policies desinged with a genuine egalitarian purpose in mind – to coax into being a society of widely dispersed ownership and power, and characterised by a far more informal pattern of work than in the past. This means that the policy-makers must now stand back from macro-economic refinements as far as possible and that they should follow the capital distribution route in social policy rather than being preoccupied with incomes.

To orthodox economists these may seem revolutionary, even shocking, steps. To Keynesians it will be 'unthinkable' that central government macro-economic policy should be passive in the face of unemployment and apparent demand deficiency. To monetarists it will be equally distasteful that the attempt at detailed control of the monetary aggregates should not have primacy over all other areas of policy. Yet to society as a whole, what looks unthinkable or distasteful from the centre has already begun to be the settled, comfortable and increasingly acceptable order. It is the policy-makers at the centre who are being left behind and failing to grasp what is happening, not the public at large.

The need, therefore, is for the energies of policy-makers to be switched in a new direction. A heavy new agenda unfolds. To this agenda, which involves nothing less than the wholesale reconstruction of policy – the policy to replace economic policy – we now again turn. In Part V we looked at the targets at which social policy should now be aiming. In Part VII we will see how these new policies and ways of approaching old problems can be woven together and linked with what has gone before, to create a new, not very tidy, but nevertheless coherent story – a synthesis of policy which connects with the way the world now works and perhaps helps it to work a little better.

PART VII

Objectives

'Now *here*, you see, it takes all the running you can do to stay in the same place. If you want to get somewhere else, you must run at least twice as fast as that.'

Lewis Carroll, *Through the Looking Glass*

CHAPTER 20

The Storms of Change

We are caught up in three great storms of change. The first is intellectual. There has been a fundamental change of mood, a rising doubt, about the effectiveness of, or even the need for, a large scale centralist approach to the organisation of society. And there is a rising recognition of the power of markets to settle priorities and achieve social progress. What Keynes and the macro-economists said markets could not and would not do, it now seems that, under completely different and new conditions, markets can after all achieve.

The second change is technological. The arguments for centralisation and scale, both in industrial activity and in administration, have been shattered by the tools and techniques of micro-electronics. Computers have acted as levellers, placing more power in many more hands and weakening the authority and knowledge monopoly of central and national governments. The explosion of information, the amazing ease of access to it and the vastly greater speed at which it is now possible to respond to it, all make widely dispersed market-based systems infinitely more flexible and efficient than ever before. They also make central government controls much more difficult.

The third upheaval is in social behaviour. Work patterns and preferences have now altered radically. So has the economic role of women, and so have the styles of family life. Attitudes to income, capital and employment have all been transformed.

It may well be that these trends have been going beneath the surface of society for years. But in the first half of the 1980s they seem to have burst into full force. They are not just the stuff of seminars and long-term speculation on social change. They present a challenge here and now to the policy-makers and the politicians. The landscape since 1979 has altered drastically. The policies and objectives of government have to do the same.[1] For the Conservatives who have been in office in Britain for the whole decade so far, one major difficulty is that their thinking apparatus as a party, which was very highly tuned in both the 1960s period of opposition and in the 1970s, has been allowed to run down to a miserable level. This is partly because of the inevitable pressures of Government, although that need not always shut out innovative thought, as the liveliness of the Macmillan government showed in the late 1950s.

A much larger part of the problem has, I believe, arisen from a confusion in the minds of the victors of 1979 about the real causes of their electoral success and the true forces at work eroding the foundations of collectivism. Those who thought that they were simply returning to the market economy and the world of classical economics, on a rebound from Keynesianism, were inclined to the view that not much further intellectual debate was necessary. The case was made. Further analysis and argument became almost a tiresome intrusion, something to be actively discouraged.

But, as we have seen, the return to market economics was never more than a part of the picture. Much larger forces were and remain at work in transforming attitudes and behaviour and carrying us forward from the assumptions of the industrialised age. The Conservatives will not recover their momentum unless they examine, discuss and build upon these changes and consolidate their position in an entirely new terrain, light years away from the consensus world of the 'seventies, which radical Conservativism rightly set out to dismantle a decade ago. They may scrape in to a third term of office simply by virtue of the inertia and incompetence of the opposition parties and the equal or even greater failure of both Labour and the centre groupings to perceive what is happening. But that is a risky course and one that could lead to bewilderment and disintegration eventually, however feeble the official opposition.

This lack of sustained intellectual coherence in the Conservative party is worrying. It has been particularly dismaying to see, for example, the decline in support for the Conservative Political Centre, an organisation once subtly positioned by the late Lord Butler near the heart of the party apparatus, yet with a licence

1. The 1986 edition of Social Trends, from the Central Statistical Office, strongly suggests that the British now see themselves as becoming more 'middle class', with 60 per cent owning or buying their homes and a boom in health food shops!

to promote adventurous thinking at all levels, as well as with responsibility to draw ideas together for the party manifesto.[1] Lately, some of the Conservative leaders seemed to have sensed this danger, and there have been attempts to give Conservative thinking a fresh coherence in the very different conditions from those of the seventies which have now emerged. The ideal of One Nation has begun to figure in speeches and the Disraelian genius for drawing the threads of the age together and of understanding and mastering change have begun to be admired again. This shift is welcome, not because there is anything to be said for a return to the consensus world of the 1970s and its associated way of thinking, for which some politicians in all political parties in Britain yearn, but because it is vital to recognise and build upon the new common ground in society.

For the makers and presenters of current Government policy the implications run awkwardly deep. Yet there is no way in which they can be escaped. The first broad one, as suggested in Chapter 18, is that national economic policy must somehow be shifted out of the front political line. This, as we noted earlier, was precisely what some people hoped would happen when the monetarists first arrived in Whitehall and at Westminster. The essence of their belief was that we could again rely on micro-economic measures to get the labour market working and ensure high levels of employment. The Keynesian interlude was over. The markets he feared could not work except in the long run, could in practice be made to work after all.

This did not, and does not, mean that there is no macro-economic role left for the central authorities to play at all. A national annual budget has to be drawn up, taxes have to be raised to finance it, judgments have to be made on how much to borrow and what effects these decisions will have, even if very roughly, on the availability of money and credit and on the exchange rate. These tasks remain inescapable, although, as suggested in Chapter 16, they are ones which the policy makers should try and delegate as far as possible to independent banking judgment by denationalising the Bank of England and

---

1. The Conservative Political Centre was set up in 1957. The author was its Director from 1964 to 1966, a period of extensive re-thinking in the Conservative Party's position and policies. No criticism is implied here of the personnel in the CPC who have worked hard over the years. But the status of the Centre and its role in policy formation has been much diminished.

pushing monetary issues away from the Treasury and White-hall. But this is very different from the kind of fine-tuning of the aggregates which the latter-day Keynesians began to believe they could orchestrate and the interventions into price and wage movements to which this overconfident belief led them. The change of emphasis in 1979 was meant to lead right away from all that and switch the spotlight on to detailed reforms to make markets operate, including the market for work itself.

However, as we have also seen, the post-1979 approach, when it came to putting it into practice, was unfortunately flawed. First, much too much emphasis (and political prestige) was placed on achieving impossibly precise targets – for monetary growth, for government borrowing (the famous PSBR) and other amorphous concepts. Second, it turned out that markets were not only ready to operate but were powered by new high-technology forces, making them break national boundaries, fragment old centralist thinking and undermine central government control altogether. Third, the realisation dawned only slowly that labour markets had anyway changed radically and that no ideal set of macro-economic policies, or 'micro' ones, could or would restore traditional patterns of full employment. Fourth, it was not at first appreciated that the central 'micro' reform needed to accommodate the new work conditions was a vigorous commitment to wider personal ownership as the key social and economic aim, *the* 'micro' reform which would allow markets to work, make the process politically digestible and inject the element of fairness, personal dignity and stability into a system which in the 1930s had been discredited for appearing to lack all three of these qualities.

Downgrading national economic policy-making and claiming far less for it (even though it cannot be dispensed with entirely) clears the way at last for the all-out assault on the 'micro' side which was intended – at least by some of us after 1979 – but which became patchy and blurred, and hopelessly entangled with wrongly conceived 'macro' policy. The new landscape at last becomes more visible. The new policy priorities must begin with an understanding of the changed work pattern and the decline of conventional employment and its culture. All the other changes of emphasis, attitude, language and actual detailed policy which the present Government should be putting at the forefront of its micro-economic reforms, flow from this initial and fundamental perception.

Specifically, we are seeing a steady growth in the informal sector of the work economy and in what James Robertson has christened 'ownwork', by which he means work which people organise and control for themselves, whether in self-employed occupations, or in essential work in the home, including Do-It-Yourself activities, or in voluntary work.[1] Not only do the work activities of more and more people fall entirely into this category, but there are increasing numbers who combine paid work for someone else (either full-time or part-time) with informal sector work for themselves.

The central policy issues are how to accommodate and encourage this new and more flexible work pattern, how to ensure that it leads, as it certainly is capable of doing, to a situation in which everyone who wishes, can lead a satisfying and well-occupied life, doing something genuinely useful and being assured, from one source or another, of the means to sustain an adequate living standard.

We have indicated that both income support from the state and a far wider spread of personal capital ownership have a vital part to play in filling in this role. We have suggested that social security benefits need to be increasingly insulated from work, at least up to the middle income ranges, both so as to encourage greater mixtures of paid and unpaid, full-time and part-time work, so as to give women freer scope for working, and also to allow older active people to continue to contribute, rather than being statistically ruled out of the workforce at an increasingly meaningless retirement point. In terms of employment policies this must mean pursuing even harder the sort of proposals espoused by the Conservative Employment Secretary, Lord Young, and his able aides, who have tried to bring their theme of 'Lifting the Burden' of restrictions and regulations in the way of greater job flexibility to the centre of the stage.[2] We probably need to go further still and develop some even more radical proposals, such as the creation of a special legal status for 'micro' businesses – say those employing sixteen people or less – giving them immunity from a wide range of employment laws and other regulations – and allowing anyone who wishes to register as self-employed for tax purposes.

1. *Future Work,* page 4.
2. See the Government White Paper, 'Lifting the Burden', Cmnd 9571, July 1985.

But, of course, it is not just on the economic front that changes are required. The whole emphasis in education and training has to be altered away from educating everybody as potential employees of somebody else towards individual resourcefulness and self-reliance. Education is rightly coming to be looked upon as a stretched process, extending throughout working life (which is itself extending), and a means of ensuring that people have the skills and aptitude to be occupied. As long as teaching implants the idea that full-time employment by some other person or organisation is the goal and that government ought to deliver it, and could if it wanted, it is also nourishing the scrapheap mentality which is the other side of the same coin. In practice, we know that governments cannot and will not deliver full-time away-from-home employment for all. Those who have been taught that they can and are then left out, naturally conclude that there is indeed a scrapheap of unwanted people in society and that they have been left upon it.

Near the heart of the problem is that children are still generally taught to look forward to 'a job' as being the source not only of self-development and satisfaction but as the sole means of livelihood as well. In other words, the conventional ethic of dependent employment and the conventional attitudes to wages and salaries are still embedded in the teaching language. Thinking about capital and ownership, and the independence they permit in order to allow a more personal control of life and work, hardly enters into the curriculum. It is all the more remarkable that despite the hostile educational ethos, the habits and expectations of personal ownership have nevertheless begun to take such a hold. But, as was indicated in Chapters 14 and 15, we are only going to see real progress towards a situation where it becomes 'normal' for families to own assets, as well as their homes, when the whole cultural climate changes. And that begins in the schools.

Industrial policy needs to follow employment measures, tax and social policies and educational reform in the same direction. Technology is miniaturising the industrial structure of advanced societies and putting smaller enterprise at the forefront of industrial and commercial advance. In effect, micro-electronics technology is forcing work away from the central area, the large conglomerate, the huge state enterprise or organisation. Work is going out to subcontractors, out to independent operators and 'intrapreneurs' and often out of the factory or office headquarters and into the home. This is the very opposite, the mirror image of the process during the industrial revolution which took people out of cottage industries and into the factory environment and the corporate business world.

The policy switch therefore has to be towards recognition of the fragmenting pattern, with tax policies in particular that cease to discriminate so heavily in favour of corporate production and against the growth of the informal sector. It is this same dispersing pressure which should shape policy towards all the old nationalised conglomerates which have been inherited from a completely different era. To some extent, it has already done so. The idea of break-up and break away, and of strongly enhanced competition, has certainly been applied in the case of bus transport and freight. One of the steps I took when Transport Minister, which gave me most satisfaction, was to authorise the sale of the National Freight Corporation to its employees, the ground work having been largely laid by my able predecessor, Norman Fowler.[1] But as we saw in Chapter 10, the monopoly ethos, the belief that services and utilities can only operate on 'a nationwide scale' is still well entrenched in key areas. It will be quite essential to change this – indeed technology will do the job anyway, although messily, if the policy-makers do not.

Agricultural and rural policy will also need to be brought together and given a push in the same broad direction. While able minds have been active in the environment divisions of the Conservative Government in responding to the new trends on the land, and in grasping that the issues of farming, land use and local employment are becoming much more intertwined, the same cannot be said on the agricultural front. There, policy remains dedicated to the treadmill of higher production, higher costs and larger farm units. That the Common Agricultural Policy of the European Community is beginning to push very timidly the other way, under intense duress, has been used as an excuse for having no coherent domestic strategy at all. It is not very surprising that Environment Ministers have been taking the lead in these vital areas, and that may anyway be the right way for things to go.

1. The sale of the National Freight Corporation to a large number of its employees was completed (from the Government side) and announced on November 8th 1981. The driving force behind the whole idea was undoubtedly the dynamic Sir Peter Thompson.

Another area where a change of policy direction must come soon is local government. There seems every reason to hope that with an able new Minister in charge, Kenneth Baker, this may happen, providing he is not frustrated by others. What most Conservatives have always wanted to see, as Chapter 11 pointed out, is genuinely independent local government, and not the sort of extended agency system, wide open to political abuse, which has so far passed for local democracy in Britain. Support is growing strongly not just for something better in its place but for arrangements through which enterprise, investment and development can be encouraged and supported more effectively at the local level. The view that towns and inner city areas should look for 'life' and the growth of activity and work from within, rather than waiting listlessly and sullenly for outside help, is entirely consistent with long-held Conservative ideals. But for that to happen, we need genuinely independent local government and the minimum of financial links with inflexible Whitehall. So far the policy attention has been on reforming the rates, but although that is an important issue, it is really only secondary. The prime aim in local government reform must be to redefine the functions of local government and design a system which gives nearly every local authority the means to perform those functions through locally raised revenues and local resources generally.

These are by no means out-of-touch, unattainable ideals about which we are talking, a hazy agenda for some distant decade. They are practicable and immediate objectives. For one thing, the policies in several instances are being switched already, or the intention is clearly developing. For another, a good many of the changes that need to come will come anyway, regardless of what the politicians do. For example, the trend to self-employment and Robertson's 'ownwork' is probably moving far faster than any statistics reveal, although in the teeth of remorseless hostility from the tax administration. Or to take another case in the industrial area, the British Telecom monopoly is already falling apart under the impact of new communications technology, far faster than the drafters of the original legislation, or some investors, foresaw. Changes in farming methods and on the land are also coming despite official policy inertia. To measure the speed at which new approaches are anyway emerging in Government policy, it is interesting to see how leading members of the Government

now depict their own objectives and to compare them with the
new landscape and its needs which we have been describing.

One of the few Conservative leaders in the present generation
who has begun to look searchingly ahead and appreciate that
the slogans of 1979 will no longer do is Norman Tebbit, the
present Chairman of the Conservative Party. He has suggested
eight key aims for Conservatives in the years ahead.[1] They are
price stability, business success, fuller employment, reduced
taxation, better care for those in need, a property-owning
democracy, more customer choice, and the maintenance of the
law and order. Let us take these in turn.

Price stability is naturally what everyone wants, not just
because inflation is an arbitrary and often cruel tax but because
attempts to control it, or try trade-offs between inflation and
unemployment, lead right back to the sort of febrile macro-
economics and debates about the Phillips curve and other aggregate fantasies which have led to such economic policy muddle
and irrelevance, as we saw in Chapters 16 to 19. Whether it is
realistic to talk of price stability as a national economic objective
for an economy like the British, is another question. The part
played by a medium-sized open economy like the British in
deciding the level of price inflation is more limited than usually
admitted. Global forces, some of which can be marginally
influenced, some part of deeper long term trends, have had
just as much to do with the general inflationary climate. So
perhaps it is right to make low inflation an objective but to
make clear that this demands much more than firm fiscal and
monetary policies at the national level, which are bound to be
very much a hit-and-miss affair anyway. They can help at the
edges but the real battle for price stability has nowadays to be
on the international level. On the national level, the best course
is to leave central monetary authorities to aim as best they can
for a rough control of the unruly monetary aggregates, in as far
as they can be measured, and to do so in a way which permits
a targetted growth of money GDP one or two per cent above
what is believed to be the likely growth in that part of actual
output which can still itself be measured. But as we have seen,
these are vague, hazy and also vastly complex concepts,
infinitely more so than the naive monetary technicians would

1. Norman Tebbit. First Disraeli lecture at the St Stephen's Club November 13,
   1985.

have people believe. To place detailed goals in this area in the forefront of a party political programme is rash, as events in Britain have already clearly shown.

The second goal mentioned by Tebbit is 'business success' both in manufacturing and services. But, again, this has to be tempered by the recognition that business is now a vastly changed animal. It must be hoped that Mr Tebbit is not just talking about corporate business and traditional business structures. The nation's business is increasingly in the hands of people who are not in factory occupations and not working the traditional forty to forty-eight hour week. There is a very great deal to be done, as suggested in earlier chapters, to change the emphasis of government policy to help the process of wealth creation and the maximisation of satisfactions in their new forms.

It is also the case that the distinction between 'manufacturing' and 'services' is melting away in everyday business life. Most physical assembly of products involves a huge service 'input'. With the growth of 'smart' electronics, the knowledge content of many manufactured products, even the apparently simple ones like a piece of furniture or a spade, is growing fast. In other words, within what economists used to call the manufacturing sector, the service part is expanding. (In many cases it is also being hived off and re-located outside the main operation, thus creating the impression that the manufacturing sector, in the old sense, is shrinking even faster than feared. This explains why sombre economic reports, like the 1985 House of Lords Report on Overseas Trade, which expressed such alarm at the apparent contraction of 'Britain's manufacturing base', should be treated with caution. They may be starting from a false and meaningless base-point.)

As for fuller employment, if this means fuller work activity, more satisfying occupations for all, then it is a realistic goal. Employment in the boss-worker sense is not going to get much fuller; however, much policy-makers may demand it. However, what Norman Tebbit has rightly sensed is that the move towards 'fuller employment' will in part be a question of perception, as extensive work done at levels which are at present invisible to central government and the statistics-collectors become more visible and acknowledged. This involves, as has been seen, not just a major switch of jobs from the black economy to the legitimate economy, but a steady growth in the informal sector of the economy, embracing both paid work, partly paid work and unpaid work.

Lower taxation, the fourth aim, is essential to accommodate both the new pattern of more personalised work which is developing and the readiness of people to use their own resources to create wealth and occupations. The tax system must allow people to provide those with whom they work with functions which give dignity and status. It must not simply siphon away the resources which would permit this to happen. Taking less away from business in tax leads more effectively than any central Government projects, or any attempts to manipulate the demand aggregates, to a fully occupied society. As was explained in Part II, we have the example of Japan to confirm that this is what can happen when taxes are low, when incentives to personal savings are high and when this is combined with a strongly imbued sense of obligation, duty and local loyalty in every citizen. In the British case, where attitudes of state dependence which have solidified over generations have to be broken, the need is for tax cutting to be used as a direct and obvious incentive to personal ownership. That is why the idea in Chapter 14 for a personal investment pool for every wage or salary earner with which income can be channelled wholly free of tax, is so important.[1] It compares with the so-called Loi Monory scheme in France, although this was a more modest affair, permitting French workers to invest up to the equivalent of £3,000 a year in equities without paying tax. But France has always been in a stronger position when it comes to small-scale capital ownership. Enclosure and urbanisation did not go nearly so far as in Britain. They left a vast layer of petit-bourgeois property owners, and even more important, their culture and outlook, intact. This has been so much the case that France has had the inner social strength to survive and prosper under even the most collectivist governments in Paris.

Another problem is that too much of the British tax system is designed and administered in a way that favours corporate and institutional investors at the expense of the individual and the self-employed. Policy should be pressing hard in the other direction. Employees should be actually encouraged to choose

---

1. A similar proposal has been put forward by the Institute of Fiscal Studies.

self-employed status. The Institute of Directors has gone as far
as to draft legislation to speed this process.

Better care for those in need is the fifth Tebbit goal. But the
key question posed by the conditions described in this book is
how far state systems can provide this care in anything like an
adequate form and how far the public authorities, either in
central government or through its local agencies, should be
asked to pick and choose, to measure needs and administer
conditional benefits. Is it really sensible to expect huge, national
organisations to provide care and good health services, and
understanding provision tailored to highly varied and individual needs? Or is not the heart of the trouble that far too
much is demanded from large-scale central provision, which
should ideally be limited to simple and general forms of
support, while not nearly enough is being made of the opportunities to provide social support on a much more local and
personal basis? These are opportunities which are becomingly
increasingly available. As capital ownership widens, so does
the scope for voluntary work either for free or on a pin-money
basis. A vast new network of voluntary endeavour is already
springing up, ready to support and substitute for the personal
social services, and to do so on a far more flexible and intimate
basis. If better care really is the aim, then it is necessary to
start swinging the whole axis of social provision away from the
traditional state systems and into a much more personalised
and localised mode. For example, mothers with young children
ought to be under far less compulsion than they are to go out
and earn a bit extra. With the central state confining itself to
the provision of a guaranteed basic income, they would then
have a much freer choice either to go out for some of the time
and bring care and help to others in the locality, or go out for
the whole time and pay someone else to look after the children,
or to stay at home, or to enjoy a pattern of life and work which
mixed and varied all these choices. So, in sum, it is not really
enough to talk just of better care through 'supplementing state
provision' through the solidified institutions of the old centralised welfare state. There has to be a full recognition of the
potential in society's new conditions for denationalising care
services and spreading responsibility back on to the shoulders
of most people in the community, after its long exile in the
soulless corridors of centralised bureaucracy.

As for health provision, the advance of micro-electronics now makes it practicable to provide far more health care services through the primary medical care team, leaving hospitals for the much more chronic and complex treatments still requiring massive capital equipment and back-up. This in turn allows services to be decentralised and tailored more closely to local and individual needs. As personal ownership spreads and incomes become less eroded by high tax and more secure at the lower levels through the underpinning provided by a guaranteed basic income, we should see a steady growth in private health purchase. Local primary health care groups should be allowed to offer services both to the private sector and under the National Health Service. The fear always used to be that state and private provision would compete with each other, to the former's disadvantage. But the opposite is much more likely to be the case. As private health insurance spreads, the resources mobilised and spent on health care should reinforce and improve the free system.

The Tebbit commitment to the property-owning democracy is obviously both relevant and welcome. Chapters 14 and 15 confirm how this must become the central goal of social policy and it is good that the Conservative Party Chairman recognises this.

As for the seventh Tebbit point 'more customer choice', the idea is right but how far is the principle of competition and the attack on monopoly going to be carried in practice? The current Government aim is declared to be the break-up of the state monopolies. In the case of telecommunications and gas transmission and distribution, the monopoly element is still very strong, although the state hold has been weakened. The danger is that from here we could head not towards decentralisation and miniaturisation of the industries in question, but to massive and cumbersome regulation of what is inherently the same centralised structure as before. The attack on monopoly and centralism must also be pursued against an over-centralised financial system for undoubtedly that, too, is very much part of the uncompetitive landscape. Deregulation of financial services and the general freeing up of the financial services sector is therefore a vital part of this policy, just as much as the opening up of the nationalised monopoly area.

Norman Tebbit rightly questions the 'valueless values of the Permissive Society' and says that the Conservative Party in Britain will be at the front of the campaign for a return to the traditional values of decency and order. But a good deal more understanding is going to be needed of the obstacles which stand in the way of this return and how they can be shifted. As the founders of British policing long ago well understood, safety in the streets depends fundamentally on local effort and co-operation. A society with a strong local consciousness and with more pride in possession is going to be ready to build on ideas like Neighbourhood Watch and to invest much more time and effort into detailed local crime prevention. So a rounded 'law and order' policy must be rooted in localism, in wider ownership and in the transfer of responsibility down and away from the institutions of centralism. Only when Conservative policy has settled how it is going to bring these elements to the fore will it then be possible to claim credibly that there is an understanding of how freedom under the law is to be maintained but not before.

The Tebbit 'Charter' has little to say on education, except that we must improve choice and standards, although, as we have seen, the shift of emphasis required in education is enormous and crucial to the whole development of society on the lines on which it is already struggling of its own accord to go. Nor does it grapple with the tortuous problems of local government reform, which have somehow to be sorted out if the essential degree of strong localism is to be permitted, and the reputation acquired by the Conservatives for hostility to local initiative and local self-government overthrown. Nor do his key points come to grips with the vital question of reorganised social security and taxation, which, as Chapters 12 and 13 show, has to be resolved if new patterns of work are to be allowed to emerge and if the new work ethic is to be allowed to flourish. Nonetheless, at a time of intellectual staleness in political circles, and of apparent extreme divergence between the preoccupations of the party political debate and everyday values and anxieties, the Tebbit attempt to map the next steps undoubtedly points in the right direction.

The serious deficiency in the whole presentation is less at the detailed level than on the broad intellectual front. Where the Tebbit goals take us, although it is not articulated, is away from a society of dependents, leaning on traditional forms of employment and looking to the centre, in one guise or another, to provide, and towards a new ethic and a new culture. It is not enough to label this individualism, or the market economy.

A new set of values, resting far more on co-operative self-reliance and far less on either collectivism or individualism is taking shape. Maybe these were always the predominant values in man's nature, lost somewhere in the ferment of the industrial revolution and its huge centralising and massifying tendencies. Or maybe the vast power which the information revolution now disperses into individual hands gives fresh opportunities for this side of people's character and inclinations to flourish where it had been prevented and diverted before.

But whatever the mainspring causes of the change, it is there for all but the blind to see. James Robertson, in an appendix to his interesting book *Future Work* has a note on the concept of the paradigm shift.[1] Taking his lead from the descriptions by Kuhn (in *The Structure of Scientific Revolutions*) of the way in which certain turning points have occurred in scientific development and in the whole corpus of scientific thought. Robertson suggests that the same kind of upheaval occurs in routine views and activities about social affairs. There comes a moment, and this may be one such moment, when the old perceptions and assumptions quite suddenly crack and crumble away, like the outward veneer of some piece of furniture that looked noble and secure while all the time the wood within was turning to woodworm and dust. Suddenly that which looked 'obvious', 'unquestionable', which 'goes without saying', for so long, dissolves in irrelevance and absurdity. A paradigm shift occurs. A new synthesis, a new grouping of assumptions resting on a new acceptance of what is 'obvious', emerges.

For many years now, far longer than most people can remember, it has been assumed that work and livelihood must unite in employment, that workers must depend on wages, that national economies are working entities (because economists from Adam Smith onwards have said it is so) and that within societies the interests of labour and of capital can be clearly distinguished and are in conflict. It has been assumed that indicators of performance and output within the national economic entity can be reliably measured and assumed, too, that they can be precisely influenced by central government policy. We have seen how all these assumptions are becoming paper thin and in some cases have ceased to be supported from beneath by reality altogether.

1. *Future Work*, page 191, Appendix 1.

We have seen how deeply misleading it is to interpret this merely as a rejection of collectivism and a return to the classical laws of economics and markets, and how market economic values, although a part of the changing scene, provide neither an adequate explanation nor a satisfying set of guilding principles for the world as it now is and is becoming. The shift not just in values, but in the way economies behave, in the way the world works, has already occurred. The new landscape opens out. Parties, politicians and policy-makers will need to show that they understand not just what we have left behind but the new conditions now crystallising in society and setting all around us. The ones who do so will connect, will see how to shape their actions and their response to fit the new landscape – and will thereby command respect and support. The ones who do not will lose both.

CHAPTER 21

Economics and Power:
Some Concluding Notes

We are suffering just now from another bad attack of economic pessimism. Yet it is possible that in the very near future we could become substantially liberated from domination by that broad and general style of thinking which is called macro-economics – and from the gloom and sensation of impotence which its practice is bound, as we have seen, to engender. Or at least we may see the increasingly implausible assumption dethroned that nations such as ours are unified economic enterprises which can be levered this way and that by the actions and controls of central government policy-makers.

If such a power was ever available to the economic strategists who have sought to rule our lives and attitudes to government for over half a century, it is surely now fast slipping from them. The inheritors of this power are not to be found round Cabinet tables or in the economic policy divisions of national Treasuries and finance ministries. Nor are they to be found amongst the ranks of the private monopolists and directors of giant corporations in whose ranks Professor J. K. Galbraith and his generation feared that influence and control over all our lives had come to reside.

The new possessors of power are many, and their means of exercising that power lie increasingly through the now revolutionised mechanisms of the market. Because micro-electronic methods can disseminate and circulate information on a scale not even imagined a decade ago, markets of millions can operate efficiently as they could not and did not do in the past. What Keynes in his time so rightly feared was not markets that worked but markets that in his world so obviously did not work. What he and others observed about them were arthritic and cartelised economic systems, called capitalism but in fact oligopoly and made up of heavily protected concentrations of wealth and of powerful institutions equipped by law and custom to preserve their monopoly privileges and prevent markets functioning.

When he peered ahead, Keynes clearly saw little sign of this order ending. We would all be dead before that happened. Indeed he half guessed that in areas such as labour organisation the monopolies would over the years become more obstructive and still more determined to prevent free markets operating. It followed therefore that Government had to step in and do what markets were incapable of doing. Government had to create the stabilising influences, the employment and the expansion which ossified capitalism, left to make do by itself, plainly could not deliver.

In this book we have tried to show that the wheel has now turned full circle. The social goals of the Keynesians remain valid but they can be reached by other methods. For reasons that were hidden by the future from the economists of the pre-War and immediate post-War period it is now possible to conclude, on the basis of strong evidential support and without resort to fanciful hypothesis, that market mechanisms can, with the aid of new technologies of unimagined force and power, adjust with efficiency and sensitivity and thus secure the desired goals of society. Maligned laissez faire acquires a new potential.

Why can it be claimed that this is so, when it was so patently not the position in the 1930s? The answers which the preceeding chapters give to this central question fall into four broad parts, one negative – the reasons why centralised industrial and economic policy-making is failing, the other three positive – the conditions in which a far more fragmented and less regimented economic order can prosper, and why and how these conditions have come about.

The negative part is, I believe, the one least understood, probably because it is the least welcome to so many deeply vested interests – interests which are not just financial and political but also intellectual. No assault is more formidable than that upon the ramparts of established academic prejudice and upon ways of thought once themselves believed to be daringly revolutionary. While of course to observe that the central economic administration of the nation is far weaker than commonly claimed, and getting weaker still, is not a way to win plaudits among its practitioners. No one thanked the small boy for the pointing out that the emperor had no clothes.

In effect we are watching, although not always seeing, the disintegration of much of the economic machinery and administrative apparatus of which the modern state has come to be composed, and of the intellectual beliefs on which it was founded. A whole structure of state activity, of central institutions and of procedures which has grown up over a period of between sixty and seventy years, roughly from the birth of modern macro-economic thinking and advice, and which has expanded massively, (its progress being of course vastly accelerated by the overriding needs of the state during the Second World War), is now becoming obsolete.

The period of growth in the size of the modern state has now ended, and a new era of contraction has begun. It is a process which is obviously without attraction for those of all political persuasions who believe that central government should be active and interventionist in economic affairs. But such people have now, as they themselves have to acknowledge, been forced on to the defensive. It is not just that the modern state is perceived, on its track record, to be a poor organiser of economic activity and social services, or to offer an inappropriate scale for the most efficient management of industrial and commercial operations. It is beginning to be accepted that the non-state can do better, that conditions have now emerged which make the dispersal of economic power away from the centre and towards independent and private activity on a much smaller scale both more practicable and more comfortable in the modern society. These are the positive forces at work which Keynes did not find in the 1920s and '30s for the good reasons that they did not exist, and which Galbraith, too, did not foresee in his imagined world of capital concentration and domination by 'the planning sector' of corporate giants.

The first key to understanding and explaining these new forces lies in the breakneck advance of information technology. It is the micro-processor, the computer and the information revolution which break everything open – cartels, state monopolies, bureaucratic domination and large-scale industrial oganisation and power. Efficient markets rely for their operation on countless different decision points and on the free flow of information. Distrust of markets in the past rested on bitter experience of market mechanisms jamming up, congealing into restrictive guilds, with protection replacing the free movement of goods and capital and concentrated wealth replacing dispersed wealth and power. We have Adam Smith to thank for implanting in us the firm conviction that this is bound to be the inevitable order of things, that businessmen will always get together to rig the market.

Micro-electronics and the circuitry of the information age were bound to change this scene fundamentally, and have done so. They stand on their heads many of the most trusted arguments about the economies of scale and the necessity for centralisation. To have full access to the information and techniques required to make complex products and organise intricate industrial operations it is simply no longer necessary to be large. A small organisation, because of its flexibility, may actually be not only as efficient but better. Information can be tapped at thousands of decision points, allowing them to survive and compete, and thus reduce the temptation to collusion and anti-market practices which Adam Smith feared would always be so strong.'[1]

The second key to understanding the new situation lies in the changed labour market and the social revolution with which it is intertwined. Earlier chapters have tried to describe the remarkable reinforcing process which is now taking place on the work scene between the demand side for labour and the supply side. A coincidence of interests in occurring between the preferences and labour requirements of modern industry and commerce, and the preferences and choices of the labour force which no social engineer would have dared predict, and which some continue to deny exists.

The new industrial structure has less and less need for full-time, on-site workers. It suits today's manufacturing and service undertakings (in as far as it is any longer realistic to distinguish the two) to organise work processes increasingly on the basis of part-time labour, flexible hours, subcontracted activity and decentralised and often quite separate support operations. Equally it seems to suit a society which attaches strongly growing importance to the home and still appears to believe intensely in the state of marriage, to adapt to these infinitely more flexible and convenient labour market, in which both partners can share work outside the home and work inside the home more fairly.

The third key to a new understanding is to be found on the

1. Adam Smith, *Wealth of Nations*. See Book I, Chapter X.

financial side. The process which is now going on apace we have described as the miniaturisation of capitalism, the spread of ownership into mass hands. The violent shake-up in the structure of financial institutions and markets, and the frenetic round of mergers and de-mergers which enliven the stock markets of the world are of course the consequences. This spreading of ownership is really the corresponding process to the diffusion of industrial power and activity and the fragmentation of the labour market (and of the labour organisations which prospered in a more centralised age). We have discussed how rapidly this is happening in advanced societies and how it can and must be persuaded to go faster and further, especially in Britain. This aspect above all, so it seems to me, differentiates today's non-collectivist social structure from the unstable monopoly capitalism which the pre-War generation understandably feared, which looked so unnervingly like the fulfilment of Marx and which seemed incapable of providing stability or full employment.

In the very first chapter of *The General Theory* Keynes emphasised that he was offering just that, a *general* explanation of how the economic and social mechanisms of society worked – and therefore how it could be influenced. What we require now is a less general theory, something altogether less embracing, more, perhaps, a set of principles for the quite different world we now inhabit, with all its incoherent and diffused variety. The need, surely, is for an explanation of the forces which make this new pattern stable and efficient, the forces which make it work when left to operate with the least possible central government interference.

We are looking not for another broad macro-economic theory to replace the last one, whether Keynesian or monetarist, but for a much better guide to micro-economics. The time is not for generalisations but for a set of maxims to which politicians and policy-makers can turn when they come to choose their priorities in new and unfamiliar conditions. What we have argued in these pages is that the macro-economists should return, as far as possible, to a more modest role in policy-making, as Keynes hoped they would in his grandchildren's time. We have argued that markets can now be allowed to work, and will work, on the basis of widespread, high-grade information, instantly accessible, in a way that was impossible and inconceivable in the past, and that public policy should aim to encourage this process through every device of deregulation, de-restriction and promotion and maintenance of competition that can be mobilised. We have argued that attitudes to work have undergone a quite fundamental change and that perhaps even our understanding of 'economic man' and his attitudes and motives needs revising in this new atmosphere. And we have argued that the financial structure of society, like the industrial and administrative structures, is fully capable of being miniaturised and is already, despite many obstacles, heading that way.

These descriptions and prescriptions clash sharply with the assumptions of post-war domestic policy-making in Britain. That is obvious. But I believe that they have a wider validity and that they apply to important aspects of the international scene as well. A limitation of this present work, amongst many, is that it does not address itself to the great issues of world security and the international economic order which overshadow all else in their long-term significance for mankind.

Yet it seems to me that the contentions that have been advanced here do indeed have relevance to these broader areas as well. The philosophy of miniaturisation is at the heart of the new defence technologies which are revolutionising strategic military thinking. The new defence concepts embodied, for example in the Strategic Defence Initiative and the European Defence Initiative, are concerned not with devastating mass-destruction but with highly sophisticated and needle-selective defence against the giant ballistic missiles and warheads of an earlier technological era. The knowledge and techniques which make up the mosaic of endeavours on which the whole SDI weaponry rests could only spring form a society which itself reflects the same mosaic and infinitely diverse qualities. Few of these advances could have been conceivable without a 'high innovation sector' which is itself the product of America's remarkably unstructured economy, with its hundreds of thousands of small-to-medium sized companies seeking out new solutions to old problems. Thus the new society which is emerging creates its own new defence systems – ones which are which are strikingly different from those suited to the more centralised and hierarchical age which is passing.

As for the giant issue of the economic development of the poorer world, here, too, there are signs of mighty change of attitude. Everywhere the old state-based 'solutions' are being questioned and a more atomised approach re-examined. It has become impossible to ignore or leave unexplained the fact that the most successful amongst the industrialising countries are those which have opted for free markets, encouraged decentralisation of economic power and eschewed excessive state control. The miracle economies of Asia provide the familiar example of this phenomenon but a study of rising Indian economic success also reinforces the lesson. Pricing, markets, competition and incentives for enterprise, often on an extremely small scale, have been the guiding principles in lifting parts of the Indian economy so hearteningly out of its previous paralysis and poverty. A whole new literature waits to be written about this process, replacing the libraries of books and acres of print about development economics which has dominated thinking for years on the subject.[1] Unfamiliar words like 'privatisation' and 'competition' are beginning to be heard in the 1960s office blocks which house the economic and trade ministries in each capital of the developing world. Soon, explanations will be called for which connect to the real and perceived patterns of business development in these economies rather than to the non-performing macro-economic policies of past decades.

A word must be said on politics. To make sense of things in the new landscape we need, I believe, to clear our minds about the concepts of left, right and centre which continue to dominate so much political comment in Britain. 'Centre' politics is not, and never has been, as some might suppose the happy medium between doctrines of the extreme. Nor is the 'Right' in any sense a coherent political grouping or movement, as the Left tends to be. As Samuel Brittan reminds us the concept of the political 'Right' comes not from English politics but from France in 1789.[2] It exists not in reality but for the benefit of commentators' symmetry. It cannot be equated with the Conservative party any more than the 'Centre' can plausibly be equated with the Liberal party or the Social Democrats.

The importance of this, so I believe, is that we should look for the true centre of politics not mid-way between the alleged left and right but at the foremost frontiers political ideas. I see the real 'centre' of party politics as being in the same position as the leader in a flying 'vee' formation. It is the centre which should lead, which should form the spearhead of political

1. The noble exceptions are of course the works of P. T. Bauer – see for instance his challenging work *Reality and Rhetoric*.
2. *Left or Right: The Bogus Dilemma*.

perception and understanding, bringing the great political parties, bag and baggage, along behind. Where one finds understanding of the new conditions we face, openness of mind towards the new policy needs of a changed age, that, for me is the political centre – not in the mish-mash middle ground of compromise with the past but up in the intellectual vanguard.

It seems to me to be inevitable that, in the dissolving and re-forming world these pages have tried to describe and explain, the parties and politicians who are least attached to state power and collective state action are bound to be best placed to cope and respond to what is occurring. For the socialists the difficulty, indeed, the impossibility, of reconciling themselves to the new realities are obvious. Only if Labour party thinkers can somehow get round the back of their party's taste for state power and central government intervention, as well as state ownership, and re-appear in the garb of supporters of the individual and the smaller groupings, can one see any hope, any relevance, for socialism, except as a temporary backlash.

For the social democrats and their allies the problems are less severe. They are, in a sense, half way to realism. The Conservatives, with their commitment both to markets and to dispersed power, and to vastly widened ownership, ought to be far the most open to new thinking and best equipped to respond to it. But, as we have seen, they, too, have much work to do, and many myths and constricting viewpoints from which to escape.

But on the whole there are grounds for such optimism. English Conservatism is a marvellously adaptable tradition, fully capable of adjusting to the new pressures and demands of society. It is healthily suspicious of the great generalisers, wisely unserious about the 'science' of economics, still clearly on the side of 'the little platoons'.[1] As long as this spirit informs government, as long as the governors comprehend the increasing limitation of their powers in the modern world, then I do not see too much to fear in my own country and indeed am confident that it will remain at the forefront of civilisation and enlightenment.

Finally, I must speak of the mind and the man who have inspired much of what is written here and whose influence on the economic and political thinking of modern times has been

1. Edmund Burke.

so massive. I was much too young to meet this man – I refer of course to Keynes – although it was my good fortune to meet several who worked with him, to learn from them and be taught by them. I have tried to imagine what he was really like. No doubt, each of us has our own 'Keynes'.[1] When I went up to King's College, Cambridge in 1956 he had been dead ten years, although his presence and spirit were so strong in the place that he might have died only the day before. How many times has one heard people wonder what Keynes would have said if he had been alive today. In these pages we have looked back frequently at what he said in the context of the thirties and I am myself totally convinced that what he offered was right for that time. A greater degree of centralism was both possible and inevitable then. My argument is not with Keynes but with those – both Keynesian and monetarist – who are missing the significance of what is really happening, who refuse to acknowledge that we have now moved into a totally and completely different economic and social environment, and that this process has, even in the last few years, been speeding up.

I know Keynes would have recognised this. I think he would have spotted the growing weaknesses of the more assertive varieties of macro-economic prescription and policy which afflict us quicker than anyone. I think he would have looked back at his prophecy about the future of economics and economists quoted on the flyleaf of this book, and he might have felt that the time of fulfilment of that prophecy, *even if it not yet arrived*, was getting very near.

1. As Robert Skidelsky remarks in his new biography, Volume One, he finds his 'Keynes' very different from that of Roy Harrod.